Ingrid Swenson & Mary Auld

Masterpieces in Pieces

WAYLAND

Introduction
page 4

1 Portraits
▪ South American artists unknown ▪
▪ Ancient Roman artist unknown ▪ English artist unknown ▪
▪ Shepard Fairey ▪ Diego Velázquez ▪
▪ Élisabeth Vigée Le Brun ▪ Augusta Savage ▪ Alice Neel ▪
page **6**

2 Landscapes
▪ Joachim Patinir ▪ Caspar David Friedrich ▪
▪ J M W Turner ▪ Katsushika Hokusai ▪
▪ Claude Monet ▪ Wassily Kandinsky ▪
▪ Georgia O'Keeffe ▪ Emily Kame Kngwarreye ▪
page **20**

5 Storytelling
▪ Ancient Egyptian artist unknown ▪ Giovanni Bellini ▪
▪ Pieter Bruegel the Elder ▪ Zheng Zhong ▪ Sahib Din ▪
▪ Joan Miró ▪ Dorothea Tanning ▪ Grayson Perry ▪
page **62**

6 History
▪ Jacques-Louis David ▪ English artists unknown ▪
▪ Paulo Uccello ▪ Farrukh Beg ▪ Ford Madox Brown ▪
▪ Pablo Picasso ▪ Faith Ringgold ▪
▪ Cristóvão Estevão Canhavato (Kester) ▪
page **76**

Gallery Matrix
page **118**

Useful Art Words
Index and Credits
page **126**

3 Animals

• Leonardo da Vinci • Ancient Egyptian artist unknown • Albrecht Dürer • Maria Sibylla Merian • George Stubbs • Tani Bunchō • Edward Hicks • Franz Marc •

page **34**

4 Still Lifes

• Caravaggio • Jean-Baptiste-Siméon Chardin • Paul Cézanne • Vincent van Gogh • Georges Braque • Henri Matisse • Roy Lichtenstein • Njideka Akunyili Crosby •

page **48**

7 Work

• Quentin Metsys • Rembrandt • John Everett Millais • Jean-François Millet • Natalia Goncharova • Diego Rivera • Jonathan Borofsky • Andreas Gursky •

page **90**

8 Play

• Ancient Greek artist unknown • Su Hanchen • Sofonisba Anguissola • Hendrick Avercamp • Francisco de Goya • John Singer Sargent • Georges Seurat • Kerry James Marshall •

page **104**

Finishing Pieces

• Claes Oldenburg and Coosje van Bruggen • Giovanna Garzoni • Dong Qichang • El Greco • Édouard Manet • Hans Holbein the Younger • Gillian Wearing • Gechū • Edvard Munch • James Abbott McNeill Whistler • John Constable • Michelangelo • Gustav Klimt • Johannes Vermeer • Kazimir Malevich • Angelica Kauffman • Paul Gauguin • Chinese artists unknown • Berthe Morisot • Benin artist unknown • Amedeo Modigliani • Yayoi Kusama • Artemisia Gentileschi • Jan van Eyck • Louise Bourgeois •

page **120**

Introduction

This book is about taking great art apart. It is for anyone who wants to take a close look at some incredible works of art from around the world and find out more about them. We have picked out details that provide clues to get you thinking about what the person who created them was saying to us. And we want to show you how – through creativity, imagination, determination and sometimes even bravery – the artist helps us to see the world in new or significant ways. We think each work of art is a masterpiece.

But how do we know when a masterpiece *is* a masterpiece? This is a tricky question to answer and leads to many more questions. Is it when an artwork from the past keeps exciting and delighting us over many years, or even centuries? Or can a masterpiece be something that was made last year, or just yesterday?

And where do you find masterpieces? Do they have to be in museums or galleries, or can they be found in other places like in a home, in a book, a tomb, a cave or in the middle of a city? One answer is just about anywhere – and, of course, all over the world. Every culture has its masterpieces.

Another question you might ask is what is the most important ingredient in a masterpiece? Is it the talent and creativity of the person who made it – even if we don't know who they are? Is the meaning and message that the artist was trying to communicate more important? Maybe it's a combination of both! Similarly, does a masterpiece need to be beautiful and celebratory or can it be difficult, sad and upsetting? Or can it, too, be both?

There are no straightforward answers to any of these questions - that's what makes them interesting! You'll find a number of famous and much-loved masterpieces in this book but we have made some less well-known or even surprising selections to give you just a taster of the world of possibility that exploring art opens up.

We would like you to read this book as though you were visiting a museum where you wander through different rooms and feast your eyes on wonderful objects. We have created eight rooms - or galleries - with each one based on a theme or subject. We start with *PORTRAITS* and finish with *PLAY*, but you can dive into this book at any point and look as long as you like. The more time spent looking the more you will discover. You'll find favourites and begin to make your own connections between artworks that stretch across themes, styles, countries and centuries.

To help you make some of these connections, look out for the *TAKE TWO* pages in each gallery, where we invite you to compare two works alongside each other. You may also want to look at the *FIND* panels which suggest connections between the galleries. In the *TAKE A LOOK AT* panels, there are suggestions which you can follow up yourself online, or in a library, taking you to works beyond the book.

After you've spent time taking masterpieces to pieces in our galleries, you can try out your expertise on some other works of art. To get you started, we have a jam-packed gallery at the end of the book called *FINISHING PIECES*. But there are many, many more extraordinary masterpieces to be seen! We could not possibly begin to fit them in to this book. The most exciting thing of all about looking at works of art is going out there and discovering them for yourself. We hope this book will be a wonderful beginning to your adventure in taking great art apart - and deciding for yourself what you want to call a masterpiece!

FIND the artworks in the book that the details on these two pages come from. Here's a clue: their shapes tell you which gallery they are in!

Portraits

We humans are fascinated with ourselves - what we look like and what others look like too. That's why we make portraits. Think of all those photos of friends and selfies we take on our phones!

A child will often draw simple figures - stick people - to show themselves and their family. These may look nothing like their actual parent, brother or sister, but to the child who drew them that's precisely who they represent - they are still portraits. A portrait need not look exactly like a specific person, just as long as it somehow symbolises that person.

We start our Portraits gallery with hands!

Cave of the Hands

artists unknown

around 8000BCE

In caves in Argentina in South America, some of the walls are covered in what looks like waving hands - as if a large group of people got together to all say 'Hello!'. These hands were probably painted more than 10,000 years ago. It's hard to imagine how far in the past that is, but it's something like 125 great grandparents ago!

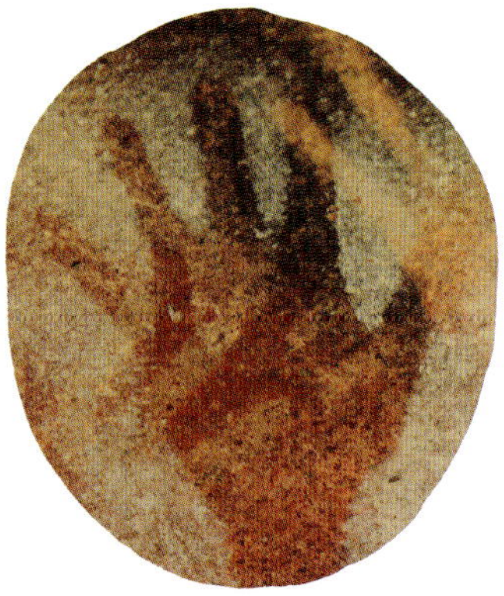

The hands look more like shadows than they do paintings, and that's because what we are seeing are stencils or silhouettes, which show the outline of the hand shapes rather than handprints.

There are different colours around the hand shapes: reddish brown, dark yellow, black and white. These were made using natural mineral pigments found in the earth that were ground down and mixed with a liquid to form a thin paste, or paint.

The paint is speckled around the edges. Can you think why? Have you ever tried blowing paint through a straw? That's exactly what these artists have done, but they used pipes made from bones to spray the paint.

And can you tell if they are right or left hands? The thumb is on the right of the hand, so that must mean they are left hands. It also tells you something else about the artists: they held their bone pipes in their right hands. They were right handed!

Sometimes the hands overlap each other. It is thought that, as different people visited the caves over the years, they would stencil their hands on top of ones from before. This creates a beautiful layering of hands on hands. It feels like we are reaching into the past to shake hands with our ancestors.

TAKE A LOOK AT the artworks of Richard Long (1945–) which are made about the land and from the land, using rocks and earth. He creates mud paintings with hundreds of his handprints in huge circles and other striking patterns.

Portrait of Terentius Neo and His Wife

artist unknown

around 79CE

A man and a woman gaze out at us in a double portrait that is thought to be one of the oldest true likenesses ever painted. They lived in Pompeii, a Roman city engulfed by ash from a volcano eruption in 79CE. The ash probably killed the couple but, amazingly, preserved their strikingly realistic portrait. It also preserved the man's name: Terentius Neo.

The Romans covered the walls of their houses with frescoes - paintings made directly on to the walls. People paid, or commissioned, artists to do this work. These pictures tell us a great deal about Roman life, from the clothes they wore to the games they played. In this case, this artist has done more than this - he has not only expertly shown us what a wealthy Roman couple looked like, but also revealed their personalities.

Terentius stands level with his wife and slightly behind her. There is a sense of equality and partnership in their relationship. It is their eyes, also on a level, that draw us into the image. Terentius looks directly at us, but his wife gazes to one side. What, we wonder, is she looking at? What is she thinking about?

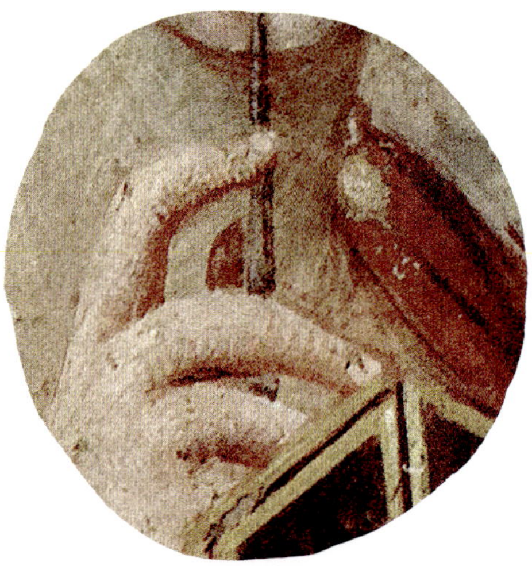

What do the objects the couple hold tell us about them? Terentius' wife carries a stylus, which the Romans used to write with, and a hinged wax tablet to write on. These say she is educated, able to read and write, unlike many women at that time. The scroll that Terentius holds and the toga he wears indicate he is important in his community, perhaps a local politician.

The artist has used some areas of paler colours to give Terentius' face shape and highlight his nose. Is it possibly broken? The artist uses thin lines to show a wispy beard, suggesting Terentius was young.

FIND *The Moneylender* in the Work gallery for an image of another married couple. Where are their eyes looking?

Terentius' wife is richly dressed and wears large pearl earrings. Her hairstyle and heavy eyebrows were very fashionable in the Roman Empire at that time. Yet her thoughtful eyes and a hint of a smile suggest she is interested in more than just fashion.

A commissioned artist may try to flatter their clients by making them look more attractive than they are. Do you think this artist is trying to flatter Terentius and his wife? What do you think they would be like if you met them?

TAKE A LOOK AT the double portrait *American Gothic* (1930) by Grant Wood (1891–1942). How is that couple positioned? What are they holding?

Take Two Power Portraits

Kings, queens, presidents, prime ministers and other political leaders have great power. But what should a powerful person look like? Fierce or friendly? Scary or cheery? In politics, portraits can be a sort of advertising – they aim to create a 'look' or 'brand' for a powerful person.

Armada Portrait of Queen Elizabeth I

artist unknown
1588

Queen Elizabeth I of England ruled her country for 45 years from 1558–1603. It was a time when a monarch was considered next to a god, an absolute ruler. The daughter of a king, she used her inherited authority with skill and intelligence. England flourished in this Elizabethan age.

This picture was painted soon after Elizabeth's navy had defeated the ships of the Spanish Armada and an attempt to invade England. It is one of the best-known images of Elizabeth I.

There are obvious clues to Elizabeth's power and wealth – her crown, her jewels and her amazing clothing. Her hand rests on a globe, and her finger points towards America – then known as the New World. *What does this tell us?*

The picture is very formal. The Queen sits up stiffly; her elaborate dress completely hides her body. Her eyes are blank and her expression is emotionless. *What other words would you use to describe her expression and posture?*

The painting celebrates both the Queen and the English victory over the Spanish, with the images of the naval battle behind her. There were at least three versions of this portrait made (by different artists) and many other images of Elizabeth were inspired by it. *What makes this portrait so effective? What does it tell us about Elizabeth's power?*

When an artist paints the portrait of a powerful person their job isn't just to show a good likeness, but also to suggest what makes that person powerful. What do these two portraits make us think about power?

Barack Obama
Shepard Fairey
2008

Barack Obama was President of the United States for eight years from 2008–2016. Unlike Elizabeth, his background was not one of inherited wealth and privilege. His power was achieved by democratic election. From a mixed-race family, he studied hard and went to a top university before becoming a lawyer and politician. He was known for his compassion and fighting for equal rights. This portrait has become one of the best-known images of Obama. The street artist and graphic designer Shepard Fairey (1970–) created it as a poster to help support Obama's first election campaign.

To make the poster, Fairey digitally altered a press photograph and simplified it into three colours - red, white and blue - to echo those in the American flag. In this unique version, he used hand-stencilling and collage of decorative papers and old newsprint to create a beautifully textured surface. *What do these choices tell us?*

The single, simple word HOPE is a direct and powerful message. But look too at Obama's head: it is tilted slightly, and his eyes look upwards. *What words would you use to describe his expression and posture?*

During 2008, around 300,000 copies of Fairey's poster were printed and tens of thousands of T-shirts and stickers were produced. The image was also downloadable from the Internet and went viral. The version we see here now hangs in the USA's National Portrait Gallery. It is truly art for the people. *Why do you think the portrait is so popular? What does it tell us about Obama's power?*

Las Meninas

Diego Velázquez
1656

The title of this group portrait means 'The Ladies-in-waiting'. This tells us that it depicts the women who looked after the Queen at the Spanish royal court where Diego Velázquez (1599-1660) worked – but it shows so much more than this. It is often described as one of the most important paintings ever made. Not because the people in it are important but because it asks so many more questions than it answers.

Can you count 11 people (and a dog)? What are they all doing? In which direction are each of them looking? In the centre of the group, the most prominent figure is a young girl wearing a light-coloured dress with a beautiful brooch. She is Margaret Theresa, the five-year-old daughter of the King and Queen of Spain.

Who is that man in the doorway at the back? Has he just interrupted this gathering, or has the artist included him for another reason? If you put your finger over the bright light that is coming from the room behind him, what happens to the painting?

Can you spot the two people in the background shown framed and out of focus? This could be another painting inside the painting, but it is a mirror and, in its reflection, we see the King and Queen. The artist with his easel is looking very intently out of the painting and along the left we can see the back of the canvas that he is painting on.

TAKE A LOOK AT the *Las Meninas* series of paintings by Pablo Picasso (see page 84) inspired by this painting. Picasso playfully explores many of the questions posed by Velázquez but also comments on events from his own day.

But who is the artist painting and where are they standing? Is it us, the viewer, or the King and Queen? We see them in the mirror at the back, which means they're standing next to us in the real world! To reflect can mean to hold a mirror to something, and also to think about something very intensely. In this painting, it means both.

This painting has kept people thinking about it and looking at it for over 350 years and it still remains a mystery. It is almost as if the artist is looking straight into our eyes and having a conversation with us about what it means to make paintings at all.

Self Portrait in a Straw Hat

Élisabeth Vigée Le Brun
1782

Why do you think that artists often paint their own portraits? Perhaps they are exploring who they are, or who they would like to be. Maybe it is a good way to practise painting difficult elements such as hands or facial expressions? Some artists may want to show off their talent. In this self-portrait, it seems the artist is doing all of these things.

Élisabeth Vigée Le Brun (1755–1842) was in her late twenties when she painted this self-portrait. She was already one of France's leading portrait painters, a favourite of Marie-Antoinette, the French Queen. There were few professional female portrait painters at the time, and she had to fight hard to be accepted. She looks confidently out of this picture, smiling.

Vigée Le Brun shows her teeth – something considered a little shocking at the time, as artists followed strict rules, which included not showing people's (possibly bad) teeth. She dared to be different – and, of course, ensured her teeth looked beautiful.

The palette and brushes she holds tell us her profession. We sense her enthusiasm for her work. She seems to be in the middle of painting as the ends of her brushes have paint on them and the blobs of paint on her palette look wet. Can you see how she has used tiny highlights of white paint to achieve this effect?

Look at how exquisitely she details the lace on her shawl. The whole painting shows off her technical skill both to possible clients and to other artists. Some people may have questioned her skill as, unlike male artists of the time, she had not received any formal training at an art school.

Vigée Le Brun wears a frivolous hat and was clearly feeling happy when she made this picture. She made many self-portraits during her life, showing off her good looks and fine clothes, as well as her success and skill as an artist. Other artists have painted themselves in a more critical and self-exploratory way. The Dutch painter Rembrandt (1606–69) made over 40 self-portraits during his lifetime, showing himself sometimes confident, sometimes serious, sometimes as a king and sometimes as a pauper.

TAKE A LOOK AT
The Straw Hat (1622–25) by Peter Paul Rubens (1577–1640). It inspired Le Brun to wear a straw hat for this picture.

TAKE A LOOK AT the self-portraits by other strong women looking directly at us, such as Angelica Kauffman (1741–1807), Frida Kahlo (1907–54) and Chantal Joffe (1969–).

Portrait Head of John Henry

Augusta Savage

around 1940

Ever since ancient times, artists have created three-dimensional likenesses through sculpture. When showing a head or upper body, they are called portrait busts. These are often large and stately, celebrating the powerful. This small (18.6 cm high) work is intimate, however, it still carries a strong message. It is shown life size here.

Augusta Savage (1892–1962) was an African American sculptor. Both her parents had been born slaves. From very poor beginnings, she fought hard to study art in New York and Paris. One French art school turned her down because some of their students refused to be taught alongside a black person. Savage's training was in the academic European tradition of classical Greek and Roman sculpture, but she applied her learning to her own heritage. She became a leading member of the Harlem Renaissance, an influential group of black writers, artists and musicians working in Harlem, New York from the late 1920s.

John Henry is an African American folk hero from the 19th century. The story goes that he was a tunnel builder who took on a machine to see who could hammer out the rock faster. He won but died soon after from exhaustion. No one knows for sure what John Henry looked like. How would you depict a young hero?

You wonder if Savage used a model for her bust, it is so life like. Look at the sensitive detail around the eyes and their unsymmetrical shape. Their expression suggests intelligence and endurance, but, since we see only the head, the artist conveys the mental rather than physical strength of an everyday hero.

What do you think the bust is made of? It reflects the light like the metal bronze, but it is, in fact, made of hard, white plaster and patinated (covered with metal based paints). This process has allowed Savage to highlight details and create a very realistic portrait. At the same time the bronze effect adds dignity to her heroic subject. Busts of famous people were often cast in bronze.

Savage's choice may partly have been cost based. Bronze is expensive while plaster is cheaper but also soft and easy to shape. Artists often make best use of the materials that are easily available. We know that Savage had made sculpture from locally-sourced clay from a very early age.

TAKE A LOOK AT the portrait bust of Martin Luther King Jr by Charles Alston (1907–77), who was one of Savage's pupils.

FIND *Hammering Man* in the Work gallery to see another three-dimensional, hard-working hero explored in a completely different way.

The De Vegh Twins
Alice Neel
1975

Two pairs of dark eyes stare directly at us in this striking double portrait of identical twins. It is painted by American artist Alice Neel (1900–84), one of the most celebrated portrait painters of the 20th century. Neel preferred her portraits to be called 'pictures of people' and painted just about anyone: artists, writers, musicians, political activists and, perhaps more importantly, her family and friends. Sometimes she painted complete strangers that she met on the street. The De Vegh twins lived next door to her.

Neel painted her many portraits in a direct and informal way. Taken together, they capture the richness and diversity of American society in her home city of New York at that time. As a single mother with her studio at home, she had to balance painting with childcare and housework. Her pictures of motherhood and of children are amongst her most striking. As with the twins here, they don't shy away but look at us as equals, with the same mature scrutiny as adults.

One girl sits squarely and firmly on the chair, while the other squeezes beside her, half perched and half leaning on the edge of the seat. Their dark hair is cut in the same style and they are wearing the same bright red pinafore dress with white ruffle-collared blouses, and white tights. There is a piece of purple painted furniture behind them, but this and other strong colours simply serve to focus our attention on the identical twins. But are the girls exactly alike?

Neel's very bold big brushstrokes not only capture the forms of the two girls, but she draws out the emotional bond between them. The seated girl on the left has her hand gently around her sister's shoulder, who is positioned slightly in front. Her hand sits slightly awkwardly in front of her. Neel's choice of this exact moment as the pose for their portrait suggests the great tenderness of the relationship between the two sisters.

Neel was in her 60s before she became properly recognised and admired by the art world. She was not interested in following the fashion of non-figurative abstract art of her contemporaries. Instead, she wanted to capture the humanity of her sitters. She was, she claimed, 'a collector of souls' – perhaps all great portraits capture someone's soul.

TAKE A LOOK AT some other double portraits by Alice Neel. Try *Two Girls, Spanish Harlem* (1959), *Linda Nochlin and Daisy* (1973) or *Geoffrey Hendricks and Brian* (1978) to start off with.

SWEET .75

Landscapes

What does the word landscape make you think about? Forests, mountains, rivers, fields and coastlines? Maybe you think, too, about the weather and the time of year. Your landscape could be bustling with people and buildings - an urban landscape or cityscape - or it could be a rural landscape such as a village with just a few houses, surrounded by countryside.

In art, the landscape is often more than the background to something else that is happening. For many artists, it is the main subject of the picture and they use it to show us very different kinds of moods and emotions. In recent years particularly, artists have wanted to explore the idea of nature and the landscape as something that we must respect and look after.

Landscape with Charon Crossing the Styx

Joachim Patinir
1520–24

One of the earliest paintings where the landscape plays a very important role is by Joachim Patinir (c.1480–1524), a Flemish artist. This isn't a landscape that Patinir actually saw, but one that was made up in his imagination. He uses his landscape to explore the nature of good and evil.

Patinir based his work on the Roman myth where the dead had to cross the River Styx in their journey to the afterlife. He used a fantasy landscape with heaven represented on the left and hell on the right. A deep blue river, the Styx, flows down the middle.

The large figure in the boat is Charon, the ferryman. The smaller man, who has just died, has to tell Charon where he wants to go: heaven or hell. Has he chosen hell? It seems so. His back is turned to the pointing angel on the left riverbank and he heads towards the other side.

Can you spot the round tower with the arched entrance, which is guarded by a three-headed dog? This marks the arrival in hell, and the point where the beautiful green garden turns into burning and parched scenery filled with frightening beasts.

FIND *The Ecstasy of Saint Francis* in the Storytelling gallery to see how the landscape is used in a religious way.

TAKE A LOOK AT the depictions of heaven and hell by Dutch painter Hieronymus Bosch (c.1450–1516).

The stream on the left is much longer than the short crossing to hell. It winds through a lush landscape of fruit trees, angels, birds and animals. Can you see in the far distance the dome-like fountain and the glittering city? This heavenly destination is much farther to travel, but the rewards are much greater.

So why has the man chosen hell? Because it is easier to get to! It is his 'choice' as he did not try hard enough to be good during his life. Patinir has created a beautiful and dramatic landscape to encourage people to lead good lives, so choosing the path to heaven not hell.

Take Two Romantic Landscapes

These two paintings of icy mountainous scenery were painted within just six years of each other, one in Germany and one in England. They are in a style that was extremely popular at the time called Romanticism. Not just artists, but writers and musicians were fascinated with the human imagination and how we can be greatly moved by the vast and infinite power of nature. The term that they used for this was the Sublime.

Wanderer above the Sea of Fog
Caspar David Friedrich
around 1818

In this painting an isolated figure stands on a rocky cliff with his back to us, dramatically silhouetted in the foreground. We can't see his face, but we sense that he is young and strong. His hair blows to the side, and he is steadying himself with his walking stick. German artist Friedrich (1774–1840) is not painting from life but has used his mountain walks as inspiration.

The blues, whites and greys the painter has used give the sense of a cold, frozen landscape. The clouds in his 'sea of fog' swirl gently around the rocky outcrops and lead our eyes into the mountains in the distance. *How do the clouds add to the drama of the image?*

The 'wanderer' stands alone and observes the immense landscape stretching out before him. He is both separate from and part of the landscape he is looking at. *Has he just reached the top of a mountain or is he on his way to climb another? What thoughts might be going through his mind?*

If this image was a scene in a film, what sort of soundtrack do you imagine it would have? How would it contrast with a soundtrack to Turner's picture opposite?

In different ways, both paintings express people's defencelessness in the face of nature's overwhelming force. Which one do you think shows the landscape as beautiful and sublime, and which one is terrifying and sublime?

Snow Storm: Hannibal and His Army Crossing the Alps

J M W Turner

1812

British artist J M W Turner (1775–1851) tells us this painting's subject matter through its title. Over 2,000 years ago the great military leader Hannibal crossed the Alps into Italy with a huge army to go to war with the Romans. We don't immediately see the figures in Turner's painting, but looking closely along the bottom, we see a number of people in violent combat. Gradually we spot many other struggles.

The Sun desperately tries to burn through the great whirlpool of snow lifted by the winds. Like Friedrich, Turner has used blues, greys and whites to depict the frozen landscape, but also to create a more threatening effect. *How do the clouds add to the drama of the image?*

Turner seems almost more interested in the drama in the sky than the battle that carries on below, yet the more you look the more fighting soldiers you see. *How do you think they are feeling? What do you think it is like to be fighting in these conditions?*

Turner effectively gave his work two names – one linking it to the landscape, one to history. *Why do you think this is? Is this a history painting or a landscape painting, or both?*

Ejiri in Suruga Province

Katsushika Hokusai
1830–32

What do you think is the main subject of this landscape? Is it the two trees that stretch the whole height of the picture? Is it the people who are walking along the zigzag path? Or is it the mountain in the distance?

This picture captures a very exact moment. Look at the clues to see what has just happened. What are those white squares fluttering about? What's that orange disk? And how about all those little dark shapes swirling around in the sky?

A big gust of wind is sweeping away what looks like a stack of papers that the figure on the left is carrying. Someone else has just lost their hat, and the leaves of the trees are being blown off the branches. Can you tell where the wind is coming from? Look at how the trees bend and how the figures hang onto their hats.

In the background is a simple triangle shape. This is Mount Fuji, the largest mountain in Japan. It sits majestically in the distant landscape, still and untouched by all the action that we are witnessing. This picture is one in a series of 36 that Hokusai (1760–1849) made. They all feature Mount Fuji from different viewpoints and in different kinds of weather or times of day.

Hokusai has created this artwork using a technique called woodblock printing, which has been an extremely popular method of making art in Japan for hundreds of years. It allows many copies of the same picture to be produced. Its very distinctive style uses strong, dark lines to outline or draw the subject. Then the artist uses only a few other colours printed on top to create a bold but powerful picture. From this method, Hokusai creates great drama and movement within an exquisite landscape.

TAKE A LOOK AT *A Sudden Gust of Wind (after Hokusai)* (1993) by Jeff Wall (1946–). His image was made digitally, combining several photographs.

FIND Albrecht Dürer's work in the Animals gallery. He also used woodcut printing techniques, but did not add colour.

Impression, Sunrise
Claude Monet
1872

This landscape is quite small (48 × 63 cm). Yet this SMALL painting made a BIG impression on the gallery visitors when it was first exhibited in Paris, in 1874. They were shocked – some people even thought that the artist hadn't bothered to finish it!

In the work on the previous page, Hokusai showed us how you might depict a landscape in certain kinds of weather. In this painting by Claude Monet (1840–1926), we are looking at how he has depicted the landscape, or to be more accurate a seascape, at a very specific time of day – early morning. The Sun is just coming up and its warmth burns through the cool, hazy clouds.

We can see two boats (or is it three boats?) floating on water with what looks like some bigger ships with masts in the background. Are those buildings in the distance with smoke puffing out of their chimneys? Sometimes it is hard to tell what is going on even if you look hard!

The artist has used three main colours: a kind of blue-grey, orange and black. In many places you can easily see separate brush strokes. Monet appears less concerned about getting everything to look exactly right. Instead he works quickly to capture the light at a fleeting moment.

How can we tell that this is a scene by the water? Water reflects objects and also light, the deep glowing orange of the morning Sun is shown reflecting in simple strokes of paint.

Perhaps you could say that this painting was more of an *impression* of the landscape, rather than a detailed observation. The artist who painted this was one of a group known as the 'Impressionists'. They loved painting landscapes outside in all weathers during different times of day and in different seasons. They were more interested in trying to capture in paint what it *feels like* to be in a particular place rather than the exact details of what you can see. At the time, this was a very different way of thinking about art – which is why some people found it shocking. This revolutionary approach to art meant that landscape painting would never be the same again!

TAKE A LOOK AT Monet's *Haystacks* series (1890–91) painted at different times of day and year. He experiments in trying to capture the effects of light, playing with colours that range from shocking pink to lush green.

Composition IV
Wassily Kandinsky
1911

This landscape is bursting with all the colours of the rainbow. It even includes a rainbow - can you spot it? There are so many different shapes and colours to pick out in this strange, vibrant painting. But what is it a landscape of?

This picture probably doesn't look like any landscape that you have seen, but look hard and you begin to spot things ... There is a yellow peak on the right, with two cones behind it. Are they trees or hills? Is that the Sun behind them?

Maybe you can find the outline of a horse rearing up on the left. Then there are three cossacks - Russian warriors - in red hats in the centre. Two have long black spears stretching to the sky.

The Russian artist Wassily Kandinsky (1866-1944) loved to paint strong colours and believed that different kinds of colour had different emotional powers. Colour, he thought, was like music, which has the power to make you feel sad or happy - he even talked about 'the sound of colour'. What do you think yellow sounds like? What about green?

Look at the blue mountain that stands out in the centre of this painting. Kandinsky was a member of a group of artists who called themselves the Blue Rider, named after a painting of a horse galloping across a landscape with a blue figure riding on it. The colour blue was the most spiritual and serene of colours for Kandinsky.

Another clue to Kandinsky's love of music and colour is in the title of the painting - *Composition IV*. The word composition is often used by musicians to describe a piece of music. It can also be used to describe how an artist arranges shapes and colours in a painting. Kandinsky wants us to look at the picture purely for the enjoyment of how the colours and shapes are arranged or composed. For him, the use of colour and shape is not just about the landscape, horses and figures that they represent.

TAKE A LOOK AT Swiss artist Paul Klee (1879-1940) who worked alongside Kandinsky. He too was interested in abstraction and music. His work *Polyphony* (1932), for example, is made up of many coloured shapes. Polyphony is music where you hear two or more tunes at the same time.

This interest and aim not to paint what the world looks like, but instead to try and paint your own emotion and feelings about what you experience, is called abstraction. Kandinsky is known as one of the artistic pioneers of abstraction.

This landscape is not entirely abstract in that we recognise actual things in it. Yet clearly Kandinsky wants us to respond to much more than this. Perhaps we could say it is an emotional landscape. What emotions do you feel looking at it?

Black Mesa Landscape
Georgia O'Keeffe
1930

Do you have a landscape, perhaps your favourite park or a garden, that makes you feel, 'This is my special place'? The first time that Georgia O'Keeffe (1887–1986) saw the dramatic, rugged mountains and desert landscape of New Mexico, in the United States, she was blown away. She immediately knew that she wanted to make this place her home.

You could say that O'Keeffe really lived *inside* her landscape, often camping or sleeping in her car to experience it at all times of day and night and in all weathers. She didn't just paint the dramatic views, she also made paintings close-up of the wild flowers and bones of animals that she found.

There aren't any people, houses or distinct features in this remote desert scene. O'Keeffe has reduced her landscape down to the elements that she loves the most. She wants to show us how simple and effective just the bold use of colour and strong horizontal planes can be. Her style of painting is similar whether she is depicting objects closely observed or open landscapes like this one.

See how she has used different colours for the hills as they go back, layer upon layer, further into the distance? In the foreground, up close, is a strip of lush green. After this the land rises up into reddish brown hills - an earthy colour that is almost like a soft velvety fabric that looks welcoming and hospitable.

Next, in the section of the picture that is called the middle distance, the hills rise up further to the mountains as the colours turn darker and more sombre, a place that you might become lost in. Perhaps this is a reminder that however beautiful, the land is a place of contrast and must be respected. And then in the far distance, the mountains turn a more majestic blue, with light hitting the snowy peaks.

TAKE A LOOK AT the landscape photography of Ansel Adams (1902–84). Like O'Keeffe, he immersed himself in nature. The two were lifelong friends and each influenced the other's work.

TAKE A LOOK AT the paintings of Mont Sainte-Victoire by Paul Cézanne (see page 52). He became fascinated with the shapes that formed a landscape. He felt they had a permanent, eternal quality, whereas what we see – the impression – always changes.

Ntange Dreaming

Emily Kame Kngwarreye
1989

The Aboriginal Peoples of Australia believe that the natural landscape and everything that it contains - rocks, plants and animals, as well as people - are all connected. The spiritual forces that created their lands, known as their ancestors, are at the centre of their belief system, called Dreamtime. This work explores the interconnection between the land and these forces.

Over thousands of years Aboriginal Australians developed a distinctive, richly patterned style of painting with natural dyes on rocks, bark and on their bodies. These were part of the ceremonies and rituals that expressed their beliefs. These patterns symbolised the outlines and shapes of the landscape, the dry earth and flooding rains, the different forms and shapes of seeds and plants. Look for the plant forms in this picture.

Emily Kame Kngwarreye (c.1910–96) was a traditional ceremonial leader in her Aboriginal community. She was also an activist who fought to keep the land of her ancestors safe from occupation by white settlers. For many years she created artworks by skilfully dying fabrics. She was also celebrated for the body decorations that she painted onto women for ceremonies.

Kngwarreye was in her 70s when she first used acrylic paints. In the last eight years of her life she made over 3,000 paintings using extraordinary patterns and colours, many coming from her earlier artworks. In this picture, she has applied the paint with her fingers directly on to the canvas. Although it may look like it is abstract art, it would be a mistake to think about it in the same way that you might think of abstract art created in Europe, America and elsewhere at the same time.

The word Ntange in the title of this painting means grass seed. This grows rapidly in Kngwarreye's land after rain, showing the ancestors' power to bring new life. The surface of the painting is covered with hundreds, maybe even thousands of dots. The colours are red, brown, yellow, black and white - natural colours of the Earth. Sometimes dots are inside others and form into tubes that seem to almost dance across the surface. We sense a landscape bursting with life.

It may be tempting to think of this painting as a kind of map, as if we are looking down onto the land. Or perhaps the artist has peered through a microscope to show us nature close up and magnified thousands of times? Although Kngwarreye's paintings do not depict the landscape in a realistic way, they are in direct response to the land and the spiritual forces that infuse it.

TAKE A LOOK AT *The Alhalkere suite* (1993), a monumental work by Kngwarreye made up of 22 canvases. Discover too other Aboriginal Australian artists, such as Clifford Possum Tjapaltjarri (1932–2002) and John Mawurndjul (1952–).

Animals

When you think about animals what's the first thing that comes into your head? Fearsome beasts, playful puppies or maybe tiny insects? We can think about the animal world in so many different ways, from animals in the wild to pets in our homes.

Many artists have taken a special interest in depicting animals. They may study them for scientific reasons as well as artistic ones, or for both. Perhaps these artists find animals beautiful to look at, but also are fascinated with their power and their intelligence. Animals are driven by their instincts - even the cutest kitten will catch a mouse!

Cats, Lions and a Dragon

Leonardo da Vinci

around 1517

One of the best-known and important European artists of the past five hundred years is Leonardo da Vinci (1452–1519). There are only 25 paintings by da Vinci in existence, but there are thousands and thousands of pages of sketches, like this one showing a collection of very active animals.

Artists' sketches are often the work-in-progress of masterpieces. They provide us with fascinating glimpses into how the artist's mind works. This is particularly the case for Leonardo da Vinci. His most famous work of art is the *Mona Lisa* (1503–1506), but he is considered a genius not only because of his extraordinary ability to paint, but because of his inventive mind and incredible talent in many subjects including science, human anatomy, the natural world, mathematics, and engineering! He had ideas for flying machines and imagined dragons. Look out for the dragon in this sketch.

Da Vinci sketched out many of his ideas. Paper was very expensive at the time, so his pages are filled with drawings, barely a centimetre is wasted! These kinds of drawings are often called studies because they were just that – the artist observing extremely closely what something looks like, not just from one angle, but in hundreds of different ways and often also in different kinds of moods.

Can you count the number of cats and lions? Da Vinci would have drawn the cats from life, which is easy to do when they're asleep, but not when they're fighting! He also studied real lions. They would have been kept in cages in Florence in Italy, where he lived at the time. He has clearly looked carefully at how they crouch and prowl.

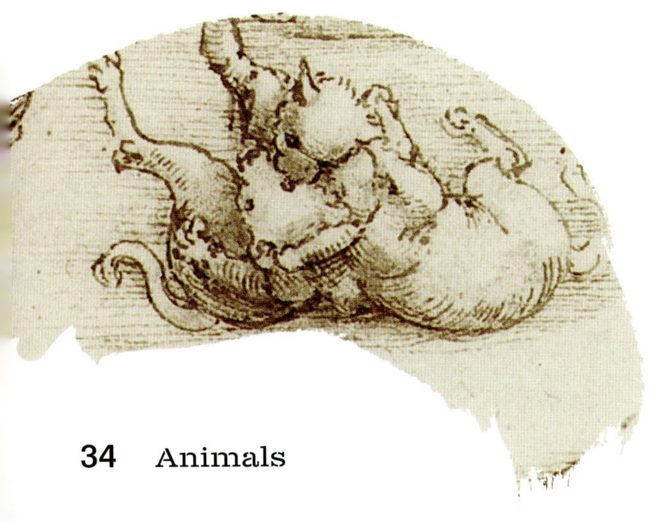

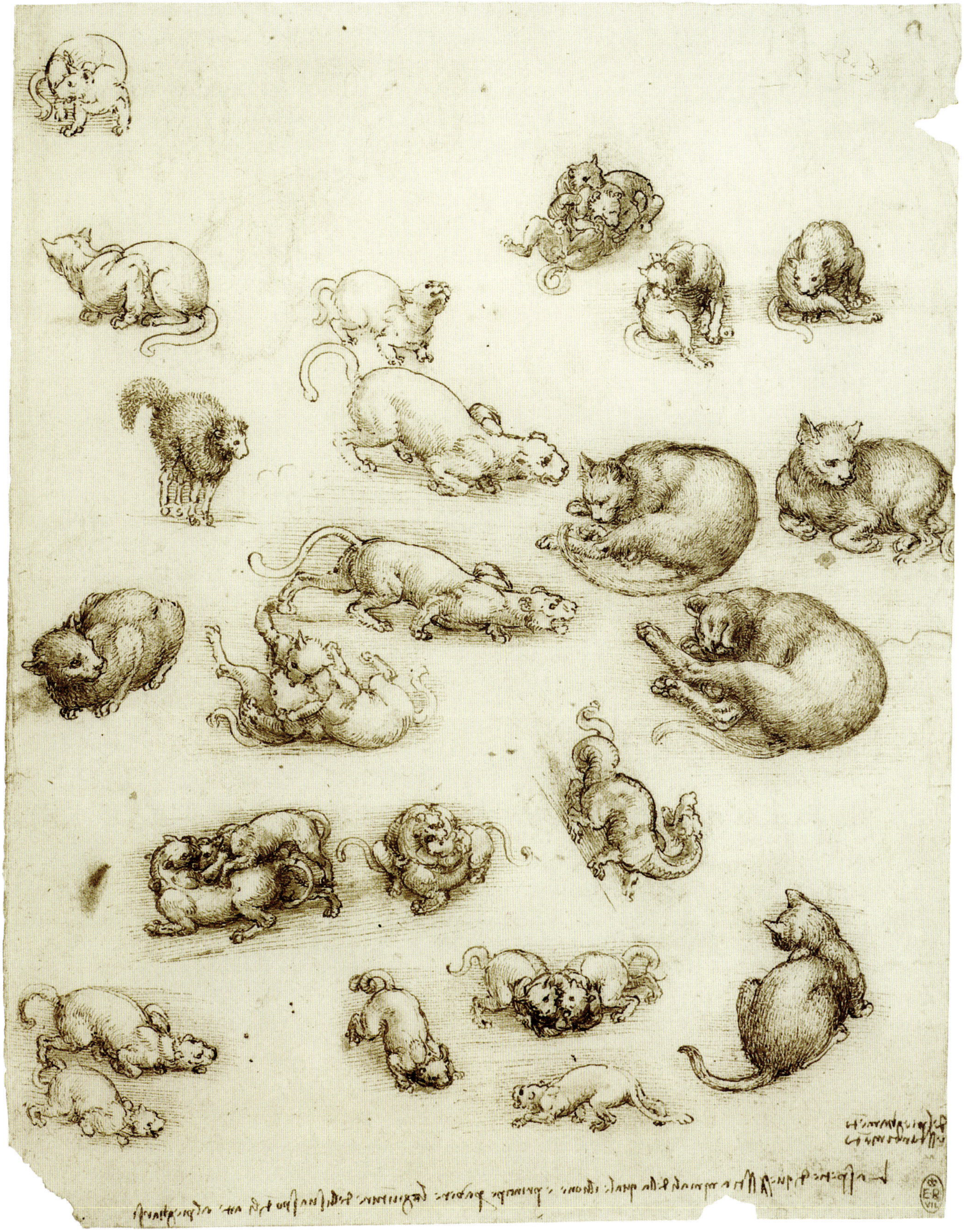

The unfinished sentence at the bottom reveals da Vinci's scientific interest in anatomy. "This animal species, of which the lion is the prince because of its spinal column which is flexible …" Yet the artist's response is not purely scientific. The animals here are so full of life, they are almost wriggling around on the page, each involved in their own moment of drama.

TAKE A LOOK AT

Lady with an Ermine (c.1490) by Leonardo da Vinci. You can see how his anatomical studies in his sketches were carried through into his painting.

Take Two Fearsome Beasts

Here are two extraordinary and majestic beasts, both dangerous to humans but also awe-inspiring. These works were made over two thousand years apart. Roughly the same shape, we immediately recognise the animals they are depicting – a hippo and a rhino – but, it seems, that's where the similarities end. The artists have created them using different techniques and styles, and for very different purposes.

Hippopotamus
artist unknown
1961–1878BCE

The hippo was made nearly 4,000 years ago in Egypt. Real life hippos are about the size of a car and were feared and respected by the Egyptians for their bulk and power. This one, however, looks, at first sight, rather sweet and is about the size of a shoe. It was discovered in a tomb. It had been placed there to protect the person it was buried with should they meet this mighty creature in the afterlife.

The Ancient Egyptians lived along the River Nile, as did hippos at the time. Hippos spend much of their time in the water. They were very dangerous to boats and fishermen. *What in this figurine suggests danger to you?*

This hippo is covered in a bright, beautiful blue glaze to represent the river Nile. It is decorated with patterns of the lotus flower, which opens in the day and closes at night, and is thought to symbolise life after death. *Why do you think the maker chose these decorations?*

The Ancient Egyptian maker of this figurine would have seen lots of hippos in nature but has created this image for reasons of spiritual belief. He would not have expected anyone to see the figurine again after it was buried. *How does it make you feel seeing this object knowing that it was made never to be seen again?*

Rhinoceros

Albrecht Dürer

1515

At first, the picture of the rhino looks like a drawing, but it is a woodcut print made around 500 years ago by Albrecht Dürer, a German artist (1471–1528). He was inspired by the news of an Indian rhino that had been given as a gift to the King of Portugal. A living rhino had not been seen in Europe since Roman times then, so this one attracted a lot of attention, rather like a celebrity today.

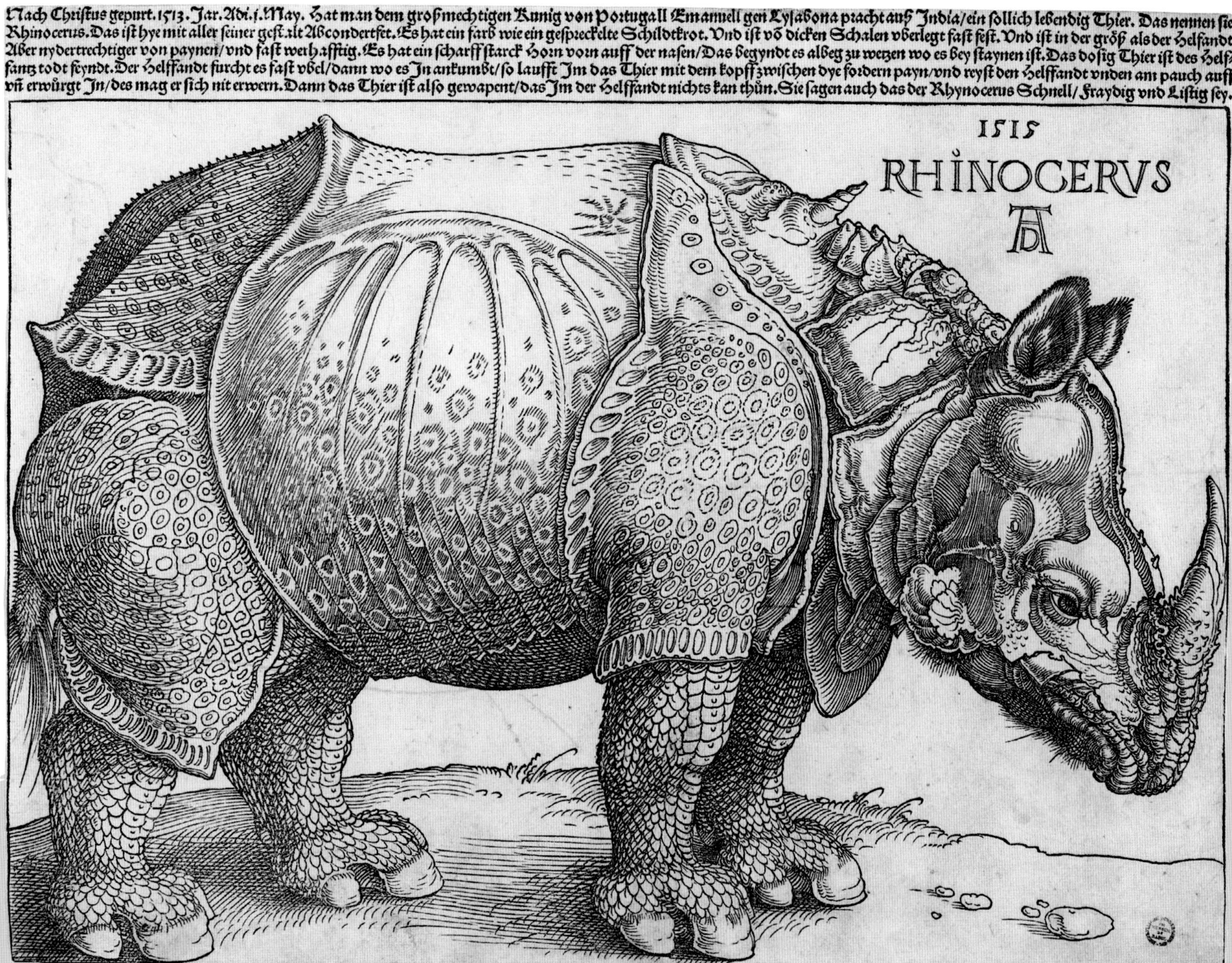

Dürer never saw a rhino in real life, but based his picture on the descriptions from Portugal. The rhino's body looks as if it is covered in sections of hard material fastened together like sheets of armour. *How does this suggest danger and strength?*

Look at a photo of a real Indian rhino and you can see Dürer got a lot wrong. His rhino's legs are covered in scales like a snake and it has fish-like gills around the head. There is a large horn on its nose, but also a smaller one, shaped like a unicorn's, on its back. *What effect does this mix of animal features have?*

As a print, there were many copies of this picture available and it became known all around Europe. For some time, many people believed Dürer's image was exactly like a real rhino. We still instantly recognise it as one. *Why do you think his image is so convincing?*

Spectacled Caiman with South American False Coral Snake

Maria Sibylla Merian
published 1705

For many of us, certain kinds of animals are less appealing than others. Spiders with long spindly legs or reptiles with scaly skin are often thought to be frightening or dangerous. But for some, such as artist Maria Sibylla Merian (1647-1717), they are fascinating.

German-born Maria Sibylla Merian loved the scientific study of insects - called entomology - and that of flowers and plants - called botany. Learning from her stepfather, she began drawing what she saw from a very early age. Making studies from nature was one of the few areas of art that was considered suitable for women at that time.

Her realistic paintings were made on vellum, a material made from animal skins. These would be copied and made into prints for scientific books. By studying her subjects so attentively, she was able to learn a lot about them - what they ate, how they lived and died. Like Leonardo da Vinci, through very close observation, she was both a scientist and an artist. She brilliantly recorded what she observed, creating works of fascinating detail.

Merian was on a scientific expedition to South America when she made this wonderful picture of a caiman wrestling with a snake to protect her hatching eggs. She travelled there with her daughter, Dorothea Graff (1678-1743), whom she had trained as an artist. The two worked closely together and some people think this picture is Dorothea's work.

The artist has clearly enjoyed observing the swirling forms, patterns and textures of the two creatures and capturing this in her painting. Despite the scientific detail, she has created a sense of movement and drama by the way she has composed the image. Yet she has shown us this battle in an unemotional way. This image is based on observation, not imagination.

Merian's works were widely admired throughout Europe, both for their scientific accuracy and their beauty. Her drawings and observations were later used by scientist Carl Linnaeus (1707–78) to support his important work on classifying animals. Her style of working, including placing animals and plants together as they were found in nature, greatly influenced the natural history artists that followed her.

FIND the work of Sofonisba Anguissola in the Play gallery. How was she limited as a woman artist in her choice of subjects?

TAKE A LOOK AT the work of Marianne North (1830–90), scientist, explorer and talented natural history artist.

Lion Attacking a Horse
George Stubbs
around 1765

In this dramatic painting we witness a lion leaping onto a horse's back, sinking its teeth and claws into its flesh. Unlike the struggle between Merian's caiman and snake, the intensity of the conflict between these two animals in this painting is terrifying.

English painter George Stubbs (1724–1806) did not go to art school, but taught himself and worked as an artist's assistant. From childhood, he was fascinated by how the human body worked, known as anatomy. He also became interested in the anatomy of animals, with a particular passion for horses. In 1766 he published *The Anatomy of the Horse*, a book of exquisite drawings, which brought him to the attention of many aristocratic clients who commissioned him to paint portraits of their racehorses.

Here he has painted the muscles and veins of the horse with incredible accuracy. There is tremendous power in the horse's neck as it twists its head sharply around, its mouth open and teeth protruded in a desperate attempt to stop the lion's attack.

You see, too, the muscles and sinews in the lion's legs. Perhaps the size of its feet and claws are exaggerated? Stubbs never saw a lion in its natural environment, but would have seen exotic animals in private zoos, called menageries. Here, lions would sometimes be encouraged to act in a violent way – something we would consider cruel today.

The landscape where the attack is taking place seems peaceful and calm by comparison. It is not one that lions would naturally live in but this perhaps was intentional. Stubbs lived at a time when the style of art called Romanticism was very popular. Stubbs wanted to explore the contrast between the magnificent and terrifying power of nature. He was so fascinated by the subject of a lion attacking a horse that he painted 17 different versions of it.

Stubbs' powerful combination of drama and physical accuracy brought a new status to animal painting. People took them as seriously as works depicting the great events in history.

FIND two artists who, like Stubbs, were interested in Romanticism in the Landscapes gallery.

Tiger Family and Magpies
Tani Banchō
1807

Tigers are considered fierce and scary, just like lions, but in this picture they are definitely playful. Maybe a bit like a pet cat with her kittens? Yet we see them in a beautiful setting watched over by a pair of lucky magpies.

Working at the start of the 19th century, Japanese artist Tani Banchō (1763–1840) was interested in many different things. He was immersed in the traditions of Japanese art, which celebrated wildlife and the beauties of nature as part of spiritual belief. He was very familiar with art from China, Japan's neighbour across the sea, and knew nature and still life art from Europe. However, he had never seen a real tiger!

Tigers are not found in the wild in Japan and there were none in zoos at the time Banchō was working. He would have seen tigers in art from China, where they are native. Japanese artists adopted tigers into their own work, where they were popular as a symbol of strength and protective power.

This tiger mother is clearly strong and her claws big, but there is something comic about her and her cubs. Banchō probably used a domestic cat family for inspiration, but he has exaggerated body shapes and given his tigers strange bulbous eyes.

He clearly drew the watching magpies from life, taking care to show the detail of their black and white plumage. He has used dark ink to highlight the pine needles of the tree and put in exquisite blue-green dots of lichen on its trunk. Paying attention to detail was an important part of making art in Japan – a meditative act that again linked it with Japanese spiritual beliefs.

In Japan, magpies are admired for their intelligence and thought to bring good luck. Perhaps by coupling them with the playful but potentially scary tigers, Banchō was aiming to make a work that brought luck and warded off evil but still made you smile. He certainly displays the great range of his talent and his clever ideas, for which he was much admired.

FIND the scroll painting by Zheng Zhong in the Storytelling gallery. How has he combined comedy and a beautiful setting?

Noah's Ark
Edward Hicks
1846

All the marvellous beasts of the animal kingdom are gathered here! But rather than being in fierce or even playful conflict as some artists have shown us, they look peaceful and friendly. The animals are all patiently lining up in pairs to board a strange looking boat – Noah's Ark.

This is the famous story from the Bible about Noah, who is asked by God to save a pair of each of Earth's creatures from a great flood. The flood was a punishment from God for people's wickedness. The darkened sky is a clue to the terrible event about to come. Hundreds of birds swirl around the threatening storm clouds, making their way to the upper window in the ark.

Below them the other animals form an orderly queue. A tiger glances round. Is he tempted by the pairs of squirrels and rabbits by his side? Perhaps, but there is no sense of danger. It seems these animals understand that they need to be kind to each other.

All the different animals are easy to recognise but American artist Edward Hicks (1780–1849) has not painted them with the extraordinary accuracy employed by Stubbs earlier in this gallery – just compare the horses. Hicks was what we call a 'Naïve' artist – he received no formal art training but taught himself art while working as a sign painter, before becoming a Quaker minister and preacher.

Quakers are a Christian group that teaches, amongst other things, to respect the Earth and all its creatures, and to be peaceful. Hicks used his untrained artistic creativity to preach this message. Noah's Ark provided a wonderful subject for him to convey his belief in people's ability to live together harmoniously in nature. The lion looks out at us with an almost human expression of calm, as sheep graze beside him.

Hicks may not have been the most accurate natural history artist, but he was a wonderful and passionate storyteller, which is why this work is still greatly loved today. Whatever your religious beliefs, this picture has a message of hope that still speaks to us. What does it make you think about?

TAKE A LOOK AT the animal paintings of French artist Henri Rousseau (1844–1910), such as *The Hungry Lion Throws Himself on the Antelope* (1905). Like Hicks, Rousseau was a naïve artist who created powerful works without formal training.

The Yellow Cow

Franz Marc

1911

The most striking thing about this vibrant painting is the intense colour of the large yellow cow. Its leaping form contrasts boldly with the reds, blues, greens and dark vertical lines. But why has the artist chosen this subject, and why has he painted it in this way?

The German artist Franz Marc (1880–1916) came from a fairly wealthy family and his father was a well-respected painter of people in country scenes. After beginning his studies in philosophy and religion, Marc decided to become an art student, bringing his interest in the spiritual into his painting.

As a young man at the beginning of the 20th century, Marc was witness to a rapidly changing world. Millions of people were moving from the countryside into towns and cities, often to work in huge factories. They laboured hard, often for low salaries. In response, many people, including Marc, became passionate about the idea of reconnecting with nature.

These people believed that the natural world offered a purer way of life. By immersing yourself in nature and getting as close to it as possible, you could achieve a certain kind of godliness, which humanity had lost. Marc aimed to do this through his work.

For Marc, painting animals in the landscape using bright colours was a way to combine his key interests – that animals are the truest and most pure of all Earth's creatures, and that colour itself has the ability to represent the most spiritual and emotional ideas. He was friends with Wassily Kandinsky and was also part of the Blue Rider group of artists.

FIND a work by Wassily Kandinsky in the Landscapes gallery. How has he used the colour blue?

For Marc, the colour yellow represents femininity and is gentle and cheerful. Why does this make an appropriate colour for a milk-giving cow? For the Blue Rider artists, the colour blue, like the mountain in the distance, represents the masculine, and is spiritual. Marc had recently married and some think that he painted this picture as a private celebration of that happy event. It is certainly a joyful celebration of an animal and nature.

Still Lifes

Artists have always made art of everyday objects – a vase of flowers, a cooking pot, a jug or maybe something that is important just to them. This kind of picture is called a still life.

Why do you think artists love to create art from such ordinary objects? Clearly it is easy to find and arrange these things, so artists have a lot more control of their subject than something that moves. Maybe, too, they enjoy looking at something closely and want us to think about it in a different way.

Artists often choose something to be in their still life not only because it is interesting to look at but also because it has a secondary meaning. Fruit and flowers may link to famous stories, for example, and what does a clock say to you? Often these choices remind us that life is not really still at all. Let's explore some of these meanings in our Still Lifes gallery.

Still Life with Flowers and Fruit

Caravaggio
or artist unknown
1601

This magnificent still life painting is an example of how artists can elevate ordinary fruit and vegetables into an image of stunning beauty. Italian painter Caravaggio (1571–1610) would have taken great care to arrange these items in his studio so that his painting would include a range of colours, textures and shapes.

What makes this painting so captivating is the artist's skill in painting strong light and shadow on objects so that they appear realistic. Caravaggio is best known for the drama that he is able to create using the contrast between light and dark. This is known as *chiaroscuro*. He achieved this by having one main light source, usually from above, as if the Sun had suddenly shone through a small upper window into a darkened room.

The object that glows the brightest is the lemon, which leads our eyes to the vase of flowers, with its white glaze shining out against the deep shadows. This area of bright colour is important to keep our eyes moving around the picture. But amongst the flowers is a butterfly, a fascinating insect that transforms from a caterpillar to an exquisitely beautiful but short-lived creature.

Many elements in the painting have important symbolic significance, which at the time would have been instantly understood. Pomegranates symbolise fertility. Walnuts can be a symbol for wisdom. Apples often represent love but also, in the Christian faith, they can mean temptation.

Near the apples are two lizards. Are they about to attack or about to embrace? The lizard can symbolise the serpent who in the Bible tempted Eve, the first woman, to eat the delicious apple, which meant that humankind would not live forever. Despite all these darker reminders, the sheer exuberance and abundance in this painting reminds us of the many pleasures to be had in our short life – and the beauty it contains.

Recently, some experts have changed the attribution of this painting from Caravaggio to an artist whose name we do not know, probably one of his pupils. Does this make you look at it differently?

The Ray

Jean-Baptiste-Siméon Chardin
1728

There are a number of similarities between this painting and the one that we have just looked at by Caravaggio. Both artists have chosen ordinary objects from a kitchen. Both have also used quite dark colours. But the paintings feel quite different. There is something very fishy about this strange still life painting!

Unlike Caravaggio's fruit and vegetables, French artist Chardin (1699-1779) has chosen food that is caught in the sea for his still life subject. In the centre is a triangular shape hanging against a stone wall. It's the ray, a type of fish, of the title. It is being prepared for cooking, with its guts exposed, which gives it a rather grisly look.

As Chardin noticed, the strange shape of the fish's head looks as if it is staring at you in a disturbing way. He uses this to great effect. Perhaps this is a way of reminding us that in order to provide food for ourselves, other creatures must perish. Objects that are connected to death, like this one, are called *memento mori* (which means 'remember you must die').

The left side of the painting is filled with activity. On the shelf are other kinds of fish and also some oysters. A kitten has just discovered some tempting treats - its back is arched and it looks surprised as if we have just caught it in the act of its theft!

The right-hand side of the painting is much calmer by comparison. A bottle, a jug, two cooking pots and a white cloth are carefully arranged. The light comes from the left. Can you see the small areas of paint where the artist has shown how light reflects on the dark surfaces?

There is a knife resting on the cloth with its handle pointing towards us – half off the edge of the shelf. Perhaps the person gutting the fish has put down the knife so that they can shoo away the cat? Or is Chardin pointing the knife towards us the viewer? Are we taking part in this picture? For a painting called a still life, there is certainly a lot of activity going on here!

FIND another picture of a kitten taken by surprise and its back arched earlier in the book. Which gallery is it in?

The Black Marble Clock

Paul Cézanne

1869

If you had to find a word to describe the mood in this still life painting, what might it be? Serious? Solemn? Frenchman Paul Cézanne (1839–1906) has created a powerful atmosphere in this still life with just a few objects. There is the black marble clock, which is the title of the painting, but what else can we see?

On top of the clock, we see the base of a pale pink vase, which is reflected in what looks like a mirror. In front there is another vase, this one is glass, but has no flowers in it. To the left of the painting is a large shell that is white on the outside and stands out very boldly against the black background. The inside of the shell is dark pink like a pair of luscious lips. Next to this is a cup and saucer, and a lemon, which adds a flash of yellow. All of these objects sit on a white tablecloth that takes up almost half the painting.

There is a feeling in the painting that time has stood still. Is it because there is something strange about the clock face? It has no hands, so we can't tell what time it is. Perhaps the artist is telling us that it can be any time you want it to be, or perhaps he is trying to paint the idea that time has stopped?

The white cloth gives the picture a sense of calm. Many areas of paint have been thickly applied – this is called *impasto*. In some places, like on the shell and the cup, you can clearly see the bold brushstrokes.

The artist has painted areas of solid black for the dark shadows in the spaces behind or underneath the table. Although you cannot see anything, there is a sense of depth. The contrast between the dark shadows and the brightness of the cloth has a quiet power. This makes the picture curiously comforting, even though its content feels very serious.

TAKE A LOOK AT
The Balcony (1868) by Édouard Manet (1832–83). Cézanne greatly admired Manet, who also used strong contrast between light and dark in his paintings to extremely powerful effect.

Monet painted *Impression, Sunrise* (see the Landscapes gallery) two years after Cézanne painted this still life. Cézanne was fascinated by the way that the Impressionists looked at the world and they inspired him to change his own approach to painting. He developed a style of painting with lighter, brighter colours using paint less thickly. He made many paintings of the same rugged landscape of Mont Sainte-Victoire, becoming increasingly focused on shape and structure. This later interest in shape can be seen here: the folds of the tablecloth also form columns that contain different elements of the composition, such as the clock face, the cup and the shell.

Sunflowers
Vincent van Gogh
1888

Wow, what a riot of yellow! Although the subject of this painting is very simple, it is one of the most loved still lifes ever made. Dutch painter Van Gogh (1853–90) must have loved the colour yellow and loved sunflowers. But why were they so special to him?

Flower paintings were extremely popular in Van Gogh's time, but sunflowers were not considered to be special, in fact, people thought them quite ordinary. But for Van Gogh, this is exactly what he loved about them – they represented something beautiful that you can find in the everyday. Look at how he has carefully shown each stage of the flower's life, from bud, through full bloom, to seed head.

You can almost feel the artist's energy when he made this painting. See all the tiny brush marks that cover the picture to represent the petals, leaves and thousands of seeds in the centre of the flower. How many different kinds of yellow can you see?

The other colour he has used is green for the stalks of the flower – this colour is made when you mix blue with yellow paint. Can you spot the small areas where he has used blue? It includes his name, Vincent. He doesn't use his surname like other artists when they sign their paintings. Perhaps this is also because he doesn't want to make things too proper or official. Just keep it simple!

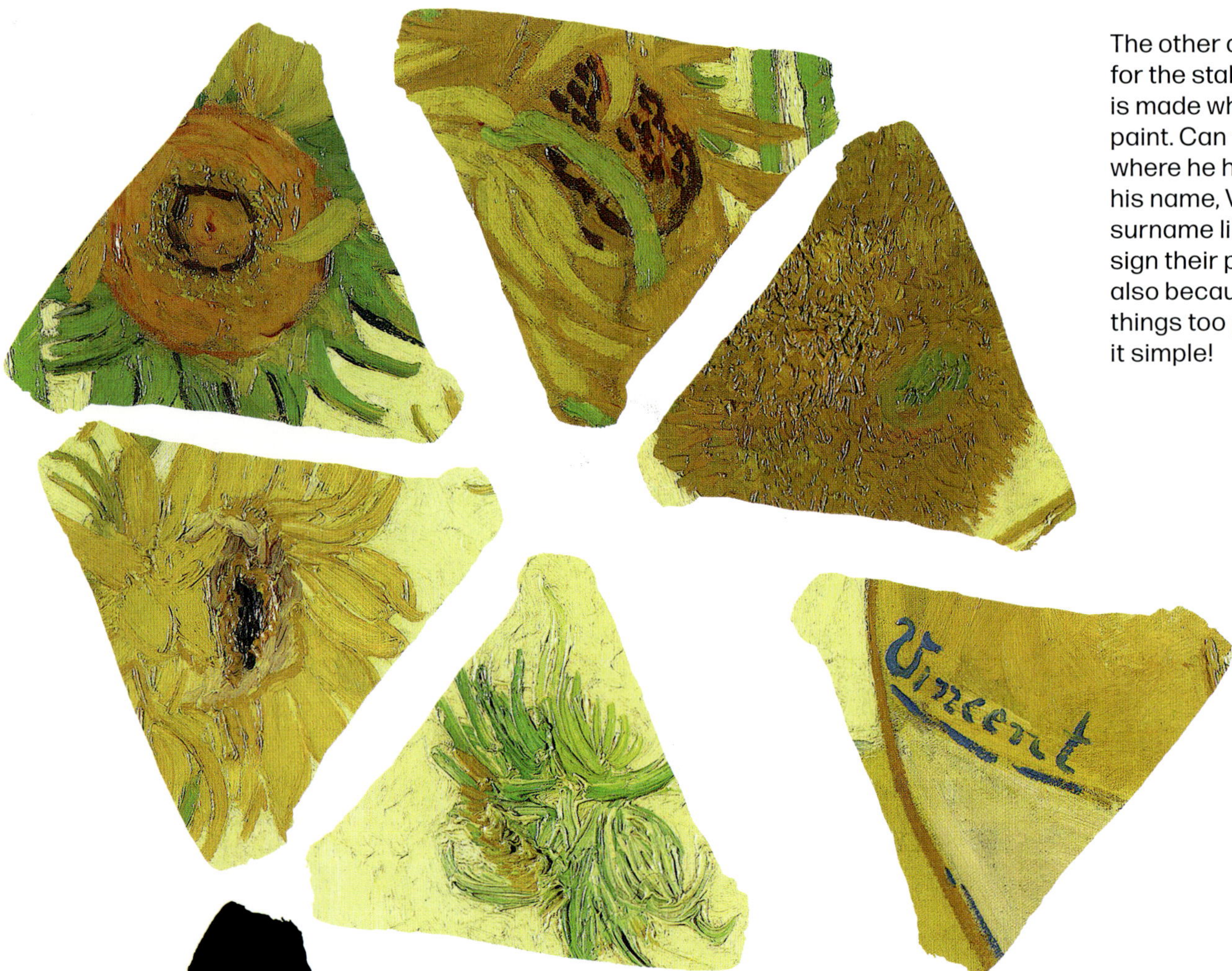

TAKE A LOOK AT
The Painter of Sunflowers (1888) by Paul Gauguin. Gauguin painted this portrait while staying with Van Gogh at his house in Arles in France.

Van Gogh loved this subject so much that he made five paintings of sunflowers and decorated his guest room with them when his friend and fellow painter Paul Gauguin came to stay. Van Gogh looked up to Gauguin and wanted him to know how much he appreciated his company and respected his opinion. For Van Gogh the sunflower was also a symbol of gratitude.

When Van Gogh died, his friends all brought sunflowers to his funeral to remember him by and show their gratitude for the wonderful paintings that gave so much pleasure.

Vincent

Still Life: Le Jour

Georges Braque
1929

We all know that pictures are flat and two-dimensional, meaning they have height and width. But we also know that objects in real life are three-dimensional. They have height, width *and also depth*. This still life finds an interesting way to explore this difference.

We have seen how an artist like Caravaggio can skilfully paint the way that light and shadow falls onto objects to make them look realistic. But French artist Braque (1882–1963) and his friend Pablo Picasso had another idea. Why not paint an object from lots of different angles all at once – looking at it from all sides? They wanted to *show us* that it is three-dimensional rather than just cleverly trick our eyes and mind to think it is. The style of art they invented is called Cubism.

Braque had great fun making this Cubist still life. There is a wooden table. We see its slightly open drawer from the front. But we also see the tabletop from a different viewpoint, as if we are looking down on it. The guitar seems chopped in two; we see it from the front and the side. The jug too is painted as a flat silhouette as well as from a higher perspective.

Braque has painted some light and shade on his apples, so they have more of a sense of reality. But he has also created a sense of collage. The wallpaper background looks stuck on. The knife looks realistic, but Braque has added a bit of shadow so it looks as if it is floating – almost as if you could pick it up and slice something with it. Perhaps the knife has been used to chop up all the objects in this picture!

Next to the knife there is what looks like a folded newspaper. The word for newspaper in French is LE JOURNAL, but that's chopped up too, so it reads LE JOUR. This is the title of the painting, which means THE DAY. Maybe this means that this painting is just like any other day?

FIND another knife you want to pick up in this gallery.

FIND some more, less playful Cubism in the History gallery.

There is a sense, with all this chopping and slicing and changing of angles and viewpoints, that Braque is just playing around. Cubism was challenging and experimental but also often playful. Together with Picasso, Braque created a new approach to looking at things that has changed the way we think about them.

Take Two Still Lifes with Fruit

These two still life paintings are bursting with strong, vibrant colours. Both artists clearly show us how much enjoyment they get from looking at their subject by creating artworks that seem to leap off the canvas and right into our world. It is fascinating to look at how they achieve this impact in their different ways. What do you think inspired these artists to make these still lifes?

Red Interior, Still Life on a Blue Table

Henri Matisse
1947

This still life features some fruit and a vase of flowers on a table in a red room where a door or window lead out into a garden. It was made by Frenchman Henri Matisse (1869–1954) towards the end of his life at a time when he was making a lot of art simply by cutting out shapes from paper. The work shows us the joy and pleasure that the artist took in creating his art. He believed our daily lives should be decorated with bright colours and shapes.

In this picture brushstrokes are free flowing, and you can get a sense of the motion in the artist's arm and hand as he applied the paint to the canvas. Matisse generates a great feeling of enthusiasm. *What sort of speed do you think he worked at?*

There are strong blocks and shapes of colour – perhaps a bit like Matisse's paper cut-outs. Yet the black zigzags in the red background change our response to these colour shapes. *How do you think the picture would look if they were removed?*

The fruit on the table – apples? – does not look exactly flat but there are no shadows on it. The light is even across the whole picture. It is the fruits' red colour against the blue and white that attracts our attention. *How do you think this picture is exploring ideas of two- and three-dimensional shapes?*

Still Life with Crystal Bowl
Roy Lichtenstein
1972

American Roy Lichtenstein (1923–97) is famous for his very bold style of art that developed soon after Henri Matisse died. He was part of a movement called Pop Art that was influenced by illustrations in comic books, advertising and popular culture at the time. He created this image working in oil paints.

In Lichtenstein's painting, there is no evidence of the paintbrush and the paint looks completely solid and flat, almost as if a machine made or printed it. He has spent a lot of time achieving this effect with oil paints. *Why do you think he worked this way?*

The strong black lines in the background are straight and meticulously painted. They come to a halt before your eye reaches the bottom of the bowl. *Why do you think he has used them in this way? How do you think the picture would look if they were removed?*

In this painting there seems to be light coming from the left, which creates highlights on the fruit, and shadow on the bowl. He has used spots of white and more black lines to give a sense of shape to the objects in this still life, yet we are very aware it is a flat picture. *How do you think this picture is exploring ideas of two- and three-dimensional shapes?*

Grandmother's Parlour

Njideka Akunyili Crosby
2016

In this still life we recognise many similar elements that we have seen in other artworks. There are things that you might find in any home, such as cooking pots, bowls and bottles, arranged on a table. Behind it there is a window, and through it we look into a garden. What is the artist inviting us to think about with these?

The title gives us a good clue to the subject matter. The artist created this image soon after her grandmother had died. She visited her grandmother's home in Nigeria to find her grandmother's table exactly as she had left it, still cluttered with her possessions. It was a strong reminder to the artist of how much she loved her grandmother.

Nigerian-born Akunyili Crosby (1983-) uses both paint and photographic transfers to achieve her effects. We can see a kerosene lamp, a food flask, a framed image of Christ and other religious objects. There is also a faded photograph of her grandmother wearing traditional Nigerian dress and smiling. Akunyili Crosby wants to show us how her grandmother's character and personality was a combination of both traditional Nigerian and Western cultures.

Through the window there is 'an impossible garden' of lush foliage of native Nigerian plants and popular non-native plants found in Los Angeles, where the artist now lives. In this way, she explores how cultures and traditions mix as people migrate. We can also make out a man's and a woman's face. Who are these people? This still life could be seen as a sad *memento mori*, a reminder of someone who has died, but it is equally a wonderful celebration of life, memory and love.

Storytelling

Everyone loves a good story. Do you have a favourite? Do you ever make up stories from your imagination or perhaps from dreams? For some artists, creating artworks is a way to tell their own, invented stories or ones told to them.

From ancient times, every culture has created wonderful myths and legends, which were told through pictures, the spoken word and later writing. Why does the Sun rise and set each day? Why do the seasons change? What happens after we die? To try and answer these big questions, our ancestors told stories that were told again and again by each generation and eventually passed down to us.

There are so many different kinds of story: fairy stories, folk stories, cautionary tales, sagas. Many are also linked to a religion. From Eid to Easter and from Hanukkah to Diwali, telling the stories about our beliefs and rituals has been one of art's most important jobs.

Painted panel of Tatiaset

artist unknown
around 825–712BCE

Ancient Egyptians had myths that expressed their belief in many gods and explored what happened to people when they died. They filled their temples and tombs with paintings, objects and hieroglyphs that retold these stories.

Ancient Egyptians believed that when people died, they made a difficult journey to the afterlife where they would be born again – if the gods said yes! This small wooden panel was buried with a wealthy woman called Tatiaset. It was not made for our eyes, but for the gods' to help ensure that she would enjoy eternal life. Tatiaset carries her heart, which will be weighed to see if she is worthy of rebirth.

Tatiaset stands on the right. In front of her, Anubis, the wolf-headed god of mummification and tombs, leads her by the hand to Ra-Horakhty, the Sun god, seated opposite. Ra-Horakhty, perhaps the most important of the gods, can help Tatiaset to be reborn in the afterlife. He is always shown with a head of a falcon carrying a red disk on its head. There are offerings to Ra-Horakhty of lotus flowers and food on the table in the centre.

Above the three figures is the sky god Horus, a falcon. He carries a shen ring and an 'Eye of Horus' in each claw, which are symbols of protection.

The storytelling is further reinforced by hieroglyphs, ancient Egypt's written language, seen here in the rectangles above the heads of the figures. Hieroglyphs evolved from simplified pictures of the things that they represent.

The person who made this object was not an artist in the way that we think of one today, more a craftsperson or artisan, whose job it was to tell a specific story using very precise images and symbols. The maker was a master of their craft, who took great care to create something beautiful – it was, after all, a gift for the gods.

FIND another Egyptian funerary object in the Animal gallery. How has the maker used lotus flowers in that work?

St Francis in Ecstasy
Giovanni Bellini
1476–78

A man in a long, brown tunic stands on a rocky ledge. Behind him is a field with a shepherd and his flock and beyond this a town, hills and a beautiful blue sky with clouds. Painted in Italy more than 700 years ago, Christians then would have instantly recognised this man as St Francis of Assisi.

This painting tells the story of how St Francis went to be alone in the wilderness, rejecting his wealth to live simply in the beauty of nature. Can you see the cave he is living in? How many animals can you spot? Francis is particularly remembered for his love of animals.

There are many Christian symbols in the picture. Bellini (c.1430–1516) has taken great care to place them realistically in the landscape. They are part of the story. A grapevine grows above the cave entrance. The wine made from these grapes symbolises the blood of Christ. Christians drink wine as part of their religious practice. On a raised desk sits a Bible – the Christian holy book – and a skull that is a *memento mori*. Further back, the donkey is linked with humility, just like St Francis.

St Francis is dressed in a simple cloak, his sandals off, and he has turned towards a golden light. Look at his face. He's looking upwards and out of the picture towards the light with his mouth slightly open. What kind of expression does he have – unhappy or happy? Perhaps stunned or astonished is more accurate?

Can you see the small wound in each of his palms? This is called stigmata, which would remind Christians who saw this painting about the story of Christ and his sacrifice. The story goes that St Francis received the stigmata while living in the wilderness as a mark of his great devotion to God.

FIND a picture from a later period in the Work gallery that is full of Christian symbols.

In this light-infused painting, the artist doesn't show a glorious cathedral with magnificently dressed people, or scenes of heaven with angels and cherubs. Instead, he tells a story of a saint standing in the beauty of nature. He is experiencing a moment of 'ecstasy' – an intense spiritual emotion and connection with God.

TAKE A LOOK AT the religious works of some other artists from Bellini's time. For example: Fra Filippo Lippi (c.1406–69), Piero della Francesca (c.1415–92) and Andrea Mantegna (c.1431–1506).

Giovanni Bellini worked in Italy during the Renaissance. It was a time when people rediscovered the culture and learning of ancient Greece and Rome and applied it to their own world and beliefs, bringing about an explosion of creativity and scientific discovery. Bellini added remarkable naturalism to religious images, glowing with wonderful light and colour.

Landscape with the Fall of Icarus

Pieter Bruegel the Elder
around 1560

Have you ever heard the expression, 'Don't fly too close to the Sun'? It comes from a story in Greek mythology and has a strong moral lesson. This masterpiece, usually attributed to Bruegel (c.1525–69), explores this story, setting it in a spring landscape, in a way that continues to excite and fascinate us today.

The myth tells how a clever inventor, Daedalus, and his son, Icarus, were being held captive on the island of Crete. The boy wanted to escape, so his father made him wings with feathers glued together with wax. His father warned Icarus not to fly too close to the Sun, but the boy ignored this advice. The heat from the Sun melted the wax and he fell into the sea to his death.

What do we see in this painting? There's a man with a plough being pulled by a horse. Behind him is a shepherd with his dog and flock of sheep. They have their backs to the sea, where there are some boats, and in the distance along the coast, a town. In the bottom right-hand corner is a man fishing, busy casting his rod into the water. None of these working men seem to notice what is happening in the sea below them. Can you see the two legs poking out of the water?

All this is set in a vast landscape, with an earthly city to the left and a heavenly city to the right. Whilst the plodding ploughman dominates the foreground, most of the people, and particularly Icarus, seem small in comparison to the sea and sky. It is similar to the effect of the landscape in Patinir's painting of the tiny man crossing the River Styx in the Landscapes gallery.

So why do you think that the artist has painted such a tragic scene of someone falling to their death in the water in this way? Why is the main event such a small part of the picture? We nearly miss it and the other people in the picture don't see it at all. Maybe this is exactly the point that the artist is making and is the moral of the story – not to be arrogant or think that you are the main focus of everyone's story, but to be humble. This was a good lesson 500 years ago and perhaps it is still a good lesson today.

TAKE A LOOK AT a short poem about this painting by American poet William Carlos Williams (1883–1963), which refers to a 'splash quite unnoticed'.

FIND the Landscapes and Work galleries. This picture could belong in either. Which one would you move it to? What details would you pick out?

Searching the Mountains for Demons

Zheng Zhong
around 1612–48

The Chinese have a long tradition of making art in ink on long scrolls of paper - perfect for storytelling. The story unfolds as the scroll unrolls, viewed from right to left. Once again, myths and legends are a popular theme. Some scrolls combine words and pictures, but this one tells its tale through images alone.

The scroll narrates a favourite legend of how the god Erlang drove demons from the mountains and saved the land from flooding. Erlang has an army of his own demons to help him. As you can see, it is an action packed adventure! Above we have focused on the part where Erlang's demons are tracking down the mountain demons.

The hunter demons are wildly ugly, but set about their work with gusto. Do you think they are funny or scary? Or both? 17th-century artist Zheng Zhong clearly enjoyed creating these colourful creatures. Chinese artists worked within strict rules, set up over hundreds of years, but you could use your imagination to draw demons.

TAKE A LOOK AT the rich tradition of Chinese landscape painting that dates back over 1,000 years. Try starting with Zhang Zeduan (1085-1145) or simply look online for 'Chinese landscape art' to begin your discoveries.

The mountain demons are rather different. They are disguised as animals, such as the two stags in this section, dragons and even beautiful women. The two women here give themselves away by their monkey children – and does one of them have some unusually hairy legs under her skirts?

All this action is set against beautiful mountain scenery. Zhong worked in 'the blue-and-green style' of traditional Chinese landscapes. Can you see how this style got its name? The landscape's elegance and muted colours throw forward all the bright colours of the characters brilliantly.

The demons, hunting and hunted, are cleverly positioned in their surroundings to give a real sense of movement along the scroll – and to tell the story. A dragon is pulled protesting from a tree and a tiger hiding in the trunk below has been spotted. Look at his nervous expression.

Zheng Zhong treated painting as a spiritual act. He did not eat before he worked and washed before he picked up his brush. Perhaps his hunger fired his imagination, giving a sense of comic-book adventure, whilst his religous rituals maintained his great respect of Chinese artistic traditions.

'Indrajit meets with Ravana ...' Illustration from the Mewar Ramayana

Sahib Din

around 1650–52

***The Ramayana* is an epic poem from India that has been popular for over 2,000 years, inspiring everything from temple carvings to blockbuster TV series. The story tells the adventures of Prince Rama and his wife, Sita. The poem is 24,000 verses long – the challenge for any visual artist is fitting all the action into their artwork.**

Sahib Din (working in the 17th century) was one of several artists commissioned to illustrate this sumptuous version of *The Ramayana*. He used the traditional Indian storytelling technique of showing multiple events in one image – a bit like a comic strip.

We follow the story by following the characters. Rama is easy to spot – he is completely blue. Sita is always dressed in blue and red. She is held captive by the evil Ravana. Ravana too is easy to find as he has many heads and arms.

At this stage in the story, Indrajit, Ravana's son, is very important. Look out for his red-spotty trousers. How many times do you see him? Start with the pink square at the heart of the image – here Indrajit meets Ravana to plot against Rama.

Next, we see Indrajit set out from the palace. Then, hidden behind a hill, we see him shoot Rama with his bow and arrow. His arrows magically turn into snakes which trap Rama on the ground. Rama has an army of monkeys, who watch helpless and horrified.

Indrajit and his followers return to the palace, rejoicing. In the red throne room, top right, Sahib Din shows us Indrajit twice: not only telling Ravana what has happened but also how his father reacts – Ravana embraces him.

FIND the work of Farrukh Beg in the History gallery. How does he use the palace architecture in his illustration?

TAKE A LOOK AT the whole of this amazing book online. Search for 'Mewar Ramayana Turning the Pages'.

The action takes place inside and outside Ravana's palace. Sahib Din uses the building's architecture to hold the story. A second storyline takes place towards its edges: in a garden in the palace, we see the captive Sita twice, on her own and with a servant who tells her that Rama is dead. Sita is taken in a flying chariot to see her husband's apparently dead body. Sita cannot bring herself to look.

We cannot read the text this work illustrates here, yet still Sahib Din manages to capture our attention – partly through the sheer busyness of the image, but also in his little touches of emotion. Like all good storytellers, he leaves us wanting to know what happens next ....

Take Two Surreal Storytellers

At first glance, these two very curious pictures seem to have nothing in common. One is filled with strange blobs and swirly shapes that you wouldn't recognise as real people or animals, but as some otherworldly creatures. The other picture looks more realistic, but the scene is most strange!

Carnival of Harlequin

Joan Miró
1924–25

Joan Miró (1893–1983) came from Catalonia in the north of Spain. The large figure in the left of the painting is the harlequin of the title – a traditional comic character who always falls in love with someone who does not return his affection. In this picture the harlequin represents the artist himself, and has a half-blue and half-red head, with a body shaped like a guitar.

When Miró made this painting, he was so broke he could barely afford to eat. His hunger made him go into a kind of daze. *How do you think this might have affected this painting? What do you think the hole in the harlequin's stomach tells us?*

The harlequin is surrounded by curious creatures. They are in a room playing instruments, singing and dancing. There is a window through which we see a peculiar star and two other shapes. *What emotions do these details suggest to you?*

You might consider this picture as a very personal story. It helps to know something about the artist to unlock its meaning, but you can also use your own imagination to interpret it. *What story do you think Miró is telling?*

Although they are very different in style, it seems both artists have painted something unreal that they have completely invented from their imagination, or perhaps they saw in a dream. Both were part of an artistic movement called Surrealism.

Eine Kleine Nachtmusik

Dorothea Tanning

1943

Like Miró, American Dorothea Tanning (1910–2012) has also filled her picture with clues that are specific to her and they are gathered together in this painting to create her own personal story. The title refers to some music by Mozart (the title translates as 'A Little Night Music') that was popular at the time. Tanning was fascinated with sunflowers. She described them as a symbol of 'all things that youth has to face ... and the never-ending battle we wage with unknown forces'.

There are two young girls. One is leaning and appears to be a life-size doll; the other's hair has blown straight upwards. The girls' dresses are in tatters. *What do these details tells us? How are they dream-like?*

The girls are at the top of a wide flight of stairs in a long corridor with numbered doors. One door is slightly open and a light comes from the room behind. *Where do you think they are? Where does the staircase go? What does the open door suggest?*

The huge sunflower is missing some petals. Can you spot them? Unlike Van Gogh (see page 54), Tanning thought sunflowers aggressive and used one here because she wanted to create an atmosphere of tension and danger. *What story do you think she is telling?*

The Annunciation of the Virgin Deal
Grayson Perry
2012

British artist Grayson Perry (1960–) loves looking into the past to make us think about how we live now. He likes retelling old stories and often uses elements from the wonderful history of art, going back centuries, for his very up-to-date artworks. There is so much happening in his pictures that sometimes it's almost impossible to take it all in!

The title is very similar to one often used by European artists of the past. It refers to the Bible story when an angel visits the Virgin Mary to announce to her that she would give birth to Jesus Christ. But in this picture a very modern looking angel is fashionably dressed and is making a different kind of announcement.

The angel is telling her business partner, Tim Rakewell, who sits on the sofa with his child, that he's now very rich because they have sold their business. This exciting news is also announced on the tablet and in the newspaper on the table.

Perry was inspired to make this work, the first of six in a series, by *The Rake's Progress* (1732–34), a series of paintings by William Hogarth (1697–1764). Hogarth had a pug dog so Perry has put one in his pictutre.

The two oval portraits show two people who were the biggest bosses in the computer software industry at the time this work was made. By showing them in this way, does Perry want us to think of them as heroes or modern-day saints? Or is he making a different point altogether?

TAKE A LOOK AT *The Heir* by William Hogarth, the first of *The Rake's Progress* series. How does Hogarth's Tom Rakewell story begin?

Many of the objects in this picture tell us the kind of home we are in – well-off and fashionable. Perry is fascinated with the decisions that we make about our lifestyle – how what we buy, wear and eat says what is important to us.

FIND *The Arnolfini Portrait* (1434) by Jan van Eyck in the Finishing Pieces gallery. Can you see the mirror and slippers that Perry refers to in this picture?

The colours are vibrant and the style of it looks more like a drawing or illustration than a painting. In fact it's not a painting at all. Perry made this artwork by drawing it on a computer, and it was then created with strands of coloured wool to make a huge tapestry that covers a whole wall.

This is an image bursting with ideas and symbols, many linked to art from the past. Perry has included a still life with vegetables and a vase with lily flowers. There is a mirror on the back wall and some slippers in a corner. Can you remember another picture in this gallery where there are some unworn sandals?

History

News today is history tomorrow – it is happening all of the time, to everyone. Even you! We are all living history and this is one of the reasons artists often explore history in their work. Of course, they may choose to focus on 'big events', like famous battles and people, but often they have an interest in a cause or event because it is important to them personally. Sometimes artists show us unhappy or terrible things from history because they want us to learn about ourselves. Other times artists celebrate a moment in history to give us joyful memories.

Sometimes, too, artists are commissioned to create a work about an historical event to celebrate it and the people involved. Their clients want to impress so these works can be a kind of advertising or propaganda. We will start with a painting that is just that.

Napoleon Crossing the Alps

Jacques-Louis David
1801

In spring 1800, Napoleon Bonaparte led his French troops across the Alps to defeat the Austrian army in Italy. This was near the beginning of the 15-year period when the great military leader of France dominated the history of Europe.

In this huge, striking painting (2.61 m high), Napoleon wears a lavish uniform, complete with a gold-trimmed hat and ornate sabre by his side. All these show his military status as a general. Napoleon's cloak billows in the wind. Strong gusts sweep up the horse's tail and mane, while clouds suggest a storm is on its way.

French artist David (1748–1825) painted this in a style that was highly fashionable at that time, called Neoclassicism. Artists took inspiration from Roman and Greek art when heroic generals on horseback were a popular subject. It is a very different approach to painting history from that of J M W Turner's in the Landscapes gallery.

We don't see any fighting, but in the background soldiers are pushing a cannon, with more troops snaking up the mountains ahead. On the rocks in the foreground, we see Napoleon's surname, BONAPARTE alongside two others: HANNIBAL and KAROLVS MAGNVS IMP. Both are famous military leaders who crossed the Alps, with whom Napoleon is flatteringly compared.

Napoleon's expression is remarkably calm. He is in total control of his rearing horse as he gestures toward his route over the mountains. We know that Napoleon refused to sit to have his portrait painted, but instructed David to show his strength of character, rather than get distracted by an exact resemblance.

In more ways than one this painting is an alternative version of the facts. In reality Napoleon crossed the Alps a few days after the troops, and he rode a mule, but this wouldn't have made such a powerful picture. The painting was originally commissioned by the King of Spain as a compliment to this new powerful ruler, but Napoleon liked it so much he had David paint three more versions.

TAKE A LOOK AT *Napoleon Leading the Army over the Alps* (2005) by Kehinde Wiley (1977–). He recreates this picture but makes key changes to create another perspective on history.

Take Two Historic Battles

These two artworks depict battles in history. They were both made close to the time of the actual events. You can see how the artists wanted to give us a sense of the conflict. There are knights in armour, soldiers, horses, shields, swords, lances and arrows flying every which way.

The Bayeux Tapestry
artists unknown
around 1070s

This tapestry is about one of England's most famous battles, the Battle of Hastings that took place almost 1,000 years ago between the French and English. The part that we see is just a small section of the tapestry (in fact an embroidered cloth) which is 58 metres long – longer than an Olympic swimming pool. Similar to a comic strip, the cloth tells the story of the lead-up to and the conquest of England in 1066 by the Normans, led by William the Conqueror.

This section shows how the English soldiers on foot are being defeated by the mounted French. It is just before the English King Harold is killed. Wounded and dead soldiers lie scattered along the bottom. *How do you react to the conflict as it is shown here?*

The embroidery is likely to have been made in England, designed by men and sewn by women. It was probably commissioned by Bishop Odo, William the Conqueror's half-brother, to be hung in Bayeux Cathedral in France. *How do you think people felt when they saw the tapestry?*

The figures are simply outlined and there is no depth to the image. Yet there is still a huge sense of movement and extraordinary detail, for example, in the armour the soldiers wear. *Why do you think this is considered a treasure of medieval art? And why is it so important to historians?*

Each work was also created to celebrate a victory. Like the painting of Napoleon previously, they have a purpose that is not simply telling the facts. However, these images, created 400 years apart, were made in very different ways.

The Battle of San Romano

Paulo Uccello
1438–40

This battle took place in Italy in 1432. Two opposing Italian armies fought for the control of a strategic port. This painting is one of three (a triptych) by Italian artist Paulo Uccello (1397–1475) that show different scenes from the encounter. Stories of chivalry and bravery were extremely popular at the time and this is an idealised version of the real event.

The military leader in the centre of the picture wears an extravagant hat. The soldiers too are in their finest armour, too heavy to fight in. It is like they are dressed for a parade. Behind them oranges, pomegranates and roses grow. *Can you find any blood? How do you react to the conflict as it is shown here?*

At that time, skilled artists were highly valued, and Uccello was considered to be one of the best. He was commissioned to paint the three pictures by a rich nobleman to hang in his palace – a bit like a tapestry. *What do you think the nobleman's friends thought when they saw the paintings?*

Uccello very carefully creates a sense of distance – known as perspective. The broken lances in the foreground appear haphazard, but a number are carefully angled to point inwards, towards an imagined horizon line, called the vanishing point. *Why do you think people were so impressed with this at the time? How do you think it reflects Uccello's fascination with the rules and science of his art?*

Babur Receives a Courtier
Farrukh Beg
1589

If your grandfather had written his memoirs, what would you do with them after he died? Particularly if he was a great ruler? The Mughal Emperor Akbar decided to have his grandfather Babur's memoirs illustrated. They were, after all, an important piece of history.

Babur was a Muslim leader from Central Asia who founded the Mughal Empire in India in 1526. He fought many battles to gain power, but he was interested in many other things – how politics worked, science, geography and history – and discussed them all in his memoirs, called *The Baburnama*. An illustrated version had to reflect this varied content.

This page shows Babur receiving a courtier. He sits relaxed on a throne, while the courtier bows to him on the left. Others kneel around him. It is an everyday scene of political life at the time. Babur's authority is clear by the position of people around him. Two guards stand to his right, but this is a peaceful scene. Notice how their weapons are covered in cloth.

There are plenty of clues to Babur's broader interests. Musicians play in the foreground. His palace is surrounded by beautiful plants (Babur wrote a lot about botany and nature). Two hares look at each other on the wall behind Babur. Above him, a hawk attacks a duck – perhaps a reminder of the strength of the man on the throne?

Farrukh Beg (c.1545–c.1615) came from Persia (now Iran) to work for Babur's grandson, Akbar, in India. The intricate patterns of flowers and foliage that decorate the palace walls come from the Persian tradition of working in miniature. They also echo the decorations found on Islamic mosques across Asia.

The Persian style seems a perfect match to Babur's wide-ranging writing and his Central Asian, Muslim heritage. Yet the energy and variety of the image hint at a new 'Mughal' style emerging in India, one that is perhaps a fitting tribute to the Empire's founder, Babur, who was powerful but also curious and wise.

TAKE A LOOK online to find other illustrations from *The Baburnama*. Akbar commissioned several versions of the book and many action-packed images were created.

The Last of England

Ford Madox Brown

1855

English artist Ford Madox Brown (1821–93) retells history through an intimate scene between ordinary people. A couple are sitting on the deck of a boat, wrapped up warm with an umbrella to shield them from the sea spray. Both have rather sad expressions looking out to the sea ahead. Behind them are white cliffs, the famous ones of Dover, England. The title of the painting suggests that they may be leaving the country forever. But where are they going and why?

When this painting was made, many thousands of people in England were emigrating to Australia and America – around 350,000 left that year. They wanted to seek new opportunities, have more freedom to make their own life choices and provide for their families' futures.

Before airplanes, these journeys by boat were long and sometimes dangerous. Passengers needed to bring as much fresh food with them as they could to prevent disease. Green vegetables are tied up on the ropes at the front.

There are more vegetables in the small rowing boat sitting on the deck at the back. This little boat has a name – *Eldorado*. This is the name of a lost city of gold, a place that you search for, but can never find.

There are other people on the boat, including some rough looking men who could be fighting, and a small girl who is clutching a green apple. But there's also the sign of another child, a baby! Can you spot the tiny hand that the mother is holding in her grey shawl?

A triangle of hands is central to this image and binds the family together. The woman holds hands with both her baby and her husband. The man's other hand, tucked under his coat, is held to his chest, suggesting love, and a warm heart.

This painting is a scene from a personal story about one family who made the difficult decision to leave their homeland to start a new life, not knowing quite what they would find. Today millions more people move from country to country for many reasons, to study, for work, for political or religious freedom, creating the multicultural society we live in today. The subject of this painting may be over 150 years old, but it is still very relevant now.

TAKE A LOOK AT the work of Dante Gabriel Rossetti (1828–82), William Holman Hunt (1827–1910) and Edward Burne-Jones (1833–98). Like Ford Madox Brown, they were members of the Pre-Raphaelite Brotherhood, who believed that art should show us what the world really looked like, working in a highly defined, detailed style.

Guernica
Pablo Picasso
1937

In 1937, during the Spanish Civil War, German Nazis bombed the small town of Guernica in northern Spain. As many as 2,000 innocent people, mostly women and children, were killed and much of the city was destroyed. When Spanish born Pablo Picasso (1881–1973) heard of this event, he decided to make a painting of it. He wanted to show the whole world the horrors of war.

Pablo Picasso was one of the world's most famous artists at that time. He was invited to make a mural for the World's Fair in Paris – an international event showcasing the best of art and technology. He chose to create this monumental painting. It covers a whole wall from floor to ceiling and is almost eight metres long – enveloping you when you look at it.

Across the surface people and animals are depicted in strong and contrasting patterns and shapes. It is in a Cubist style (see page 56) but without any colour. It is thought that Picasso wanted us to see the painting like a newspaper image, which at the time was only in black and white.

On the left a wailing woman grieves for the dead child in her arms. Her tongue is shown as a dagger. She is watched over by a bull, a symbol of Spain, with eyes wide open, as a witness to the slaughter of innocence.

The tormented horse in the centre symbolised for Picasso the suffering of Guernica. Above its head a light bulb blazes to create the shape of an eye – witnessing the tragedy. Another light source, this time a candle, appears to be held by a figure that sweeps in through a window at the right.

TAKE A LOOK AT at *War* (1921–22), a series of woodcuts by Käthe Kollwitz (1867–1945) which explore the human tragedy and impact of the First World War (1914–18) on ordinary people without showing actual combat. Other artists who are well-known for their powerful depictions of the impact of war are Francisco de Goya (see page 112), George Grosz (1893–1959) and sculptor Charles Sargeant Jagger (1885–1934).

Next to this, another figure, beneath a window, has arms stretched high and head back as if crying for help. At the bottom a dead soldier's severed arm holds a broken sword from which a flower grows. Everywhere in the painting is anguish.

The response from the public in Paris to Picasso's depiction of the impact of war was extraordinary. Picasso won the Grand Prize for art at the Fair. *Guernica* then travelled around the world to be seen by millions. It is often considered the most important anti-war painting ever made.

The Sunflower Quilting Bee at Arles

Faith Ringgold
1991

Many artists choose to explore their own, personal history through their artworks. This can be a way to tell us about the world today, and also a way to explore their life as part of history. Importantly, too, artists can use their own stories to contribute to change – to make history.

After graduating from art school in 1959, African American artist Faith Ringgold (1930–) travelled to Europe to see first-hand the art that inspired her. She was struck by the fact that there were hardly any images of or by people who were not white. Around this time, she became involved in the Civil Rights Movement in the United States when many black people demonstrated peacefully for racial equality.

This vibrant painting is a celebration of Ringgold's love for painting and a tribute to eight powerful African American women from history that she deeply admired as freedom fighters, educators and workers for positive change. From upper left they are Madam Walker, Sojourner Truth, Ida Wells, Fannie Lou Hamer, Harriet Tubman, Rosa Parks, Mary McLeod Bethune, and Ella Baker.

The women are in a field of sunflowers, sitting around a patchwork cloth of sunflowers. From the title we know that they are making this at a quilting bee – a tradition where women gather together to sew. For Ringgold, this collective way of working is highly creative and fulfils our instinct to unite and share. And for her it is also the opposite of the usual idea of the artist painting alone in his or her studio.

The title also tells us where this is taking place, Arles, in the south of France. This is where Vincent van Gogh lived for a time and when, as we learned earlier, he made a number of paintings of sunflowers. And look! There he is, presenting the women with one of his vases and flowers that for him symbolised gratitude.

In a joyous way, Ringgold's painting points us towards both the history of the American Civil Rights Movement and art history. In this painting we discover humanity and gratitude all rolled into one.

FIND another woman artist in the Storytelling gallery that uses a sunflower in her painting but with a more mysterious meaning.

TAKE A LOOK AT *The Dinner Party* by Judy Chicago (1939–). This huge sculpture in the shape of a triangular table celebrates powerful mythical and historical women – including many shown here!

Throne of Weapons

Cristóvão Estevão Canhavato (Kester)
2001

You would be right if you said that this looked like a chair, but you would also be right if you said it looked like a sculpture. The artist who made it, Kester, wanted us to think about it as both – and to create art from his country's history.

At first glance, the chair's strong angles and shapes make a very striking impression. Then you realise what these are made from – guns, rifles and other weapons of war have been cut up and welded together to create this extraordinary chair. As the title tells us, it is a throne – a seat fit for a noble king or a chief to be used at ceremonies. However, the materials that Kester used do not suggest celebration but death and destruction.

Like many of the artworks in our History gallery, it is important to think about *when* and *why* the artwork has been made as a way of thinking about *how* the artist has chosen to make it.

Kester (1966–) lives in Mozambique, which like many African countries had been colonised and run for hundreds of years by a European country, in this case by Portugal. After a long struggle, the country gained independence in 1975 but there were still many arguments about how it should be run and various groups battled for power.

A devastating civil war broke out, fuelled by arms supplied by other countries wanting to influence the result and by arms dealers looking to make a profit. The weapons in this throne come from all over the world. In the long years of war, over a million people were killed and many more became refugees.

When peace was finally declared in 1992, people needed to find ways to come together again and rebuild their lives after the horror of war. As part of the peace and reconciliation process, people handed in hundreds of thousands of weapons and in return were given practical tools such as hoes, sewing machines, bicycles and roofing materials.

Kester is one of a group of artists who makes sculptures with these weapons. He sees these artworks as an important way to commemorate the tragedy of war, but also to show the potential for hope. To create something new and celebratory out of something which is normally associated with destruction and suffering is a way to heal the wounds of the people and the country. Can you see a face on one of the rifle butts, formed by two screw holes and the strap hole? The artist wanted his throne to be a memorial to both human tragedy and human endurance.

FIND (or rather look back at) the different works of art in this History gallery. How are they, in their own way, a part of history? How are all artists making history?

Work

Much of our lives are taken up by work in one form or another. We start young with work linked to school and maybe chores at home. As adults, we will work to 'earn a living' - to make money necessary to pay for our daily life. Yet within the world of work, there is a huge variety of experiences that artists often explore in their 'work'.

For many people work is enjoyable and rewarding, because it pays a salary and is also stimulating. It provides a sense of pride and achievement. For others, work can be boring, poorly paid and exhausting. Sometimes, what is a hard physical slog for one person is pure pleasure for another!

Money connects these different kinds of work. It was invented as a way to work out the value of everything, including labour. Money enables people to trade what they have (including their time) for what they want or need. And it is with money that we begin and end our gallery about Work.

The Moneylender and His Wife

Quentin Metsys
1514

In this wonderfully detailed painting, a man holds a pair of scales in his left hand and a coin in his right. The title tells us that he is a moneylender - a sort of banker. Moneylenders did well in the busy trading cities and ports at that time, but, like the bankers of today, they were not always popular or their work admired.

On the table, the moneylender has a pile of gold coins, jewellery and some pearls gleaming on a little black cushion. The woman looks up from the religious book that she is reading. Her mind is distracted away from her spiritual thoughts and is drawn to the gleaming wealth in front of her.

Behind the couple on the shelf are various items. As in a still life, each has a symbolic significance. Glass rosary beads hang beneath a bottle of water, representing purity. These are in contrast to the apple, which refers to how we are tempted by things we can't have, and also the snuffed-out candle, which reminds us that our lives are only temporary.

Flemish artist Quentin Metsys (1466–1530) gives us two views out of the room where the couple are sitting. Through a door at the back, we can see an older man speaking earnestly to a younger man. And reflected in the small round mirror on the table we see a man reading, with a view out of the window behind him. Are these just glimpses into other spaces or does the artist want to tell us something else?

The scales that the man holds suggest that everything is in the balance - are the couple also being weighed and judged? Perhaps the message here is that although great wealth enables us to afford luxuries, it cannot replace a happy and spiritual life.

FIND a work by Jan van Eyck, also a Flemish artist, in the Finishing Pieces gallery. Van Eyck is thought to have influenced Metsys. Can you see why?

FIND some of the other works in this book that feature mirrors. How are the artists using mirrors and reflections to explore their themes?

The Anatomy Lesson of Dr Nicolaes Tulp

Rembrandt

1632

This striking group portrait focuses on a medical lesson in action. When up-and-coming artist Rembrandt was 25 years old, he was commissioned to paint the Guild of Surgeons in Amsterdam. He decided to give the painting some drama by showing one of its leading members at work.

Dr Nicolaes Tulp is performing an autopsy, in the company of seven other medical surgeons. They are gathered around a corpse of a man lying on a table – his left arm and hand have been carefully cut open, or dissected, for examination. All this action is illuminated by a strong source of light from the left.

A guild is a group formed by craftsmen or professionals to set standards and agree working practices. At the time this was painted, guilds in Holland were rich and powerful. The members of the Guild of Surgeons all paid to be in this picture, so they wanted to be sure to be remembered! The name of each man appears written on a piece of paper held by the figure in the centre.

Each man's portrait is strikingly realistic. Rembrandt has made them look serious and professional but broke with tradition with the active setting. As well as the surgeons, an audience of students and paying members of the public would be watching this gruesome event. But Rembrandt has made up part of this drama – Dr Tulp would not have, in fact, performed the autopsy himself.

TAKE A LOOK AT the largest and perhaps most ambitious group portrait by Rembrandt, *The Night Watch* (1642). Again, see how the artist has carefully painted the light to focus our attention.

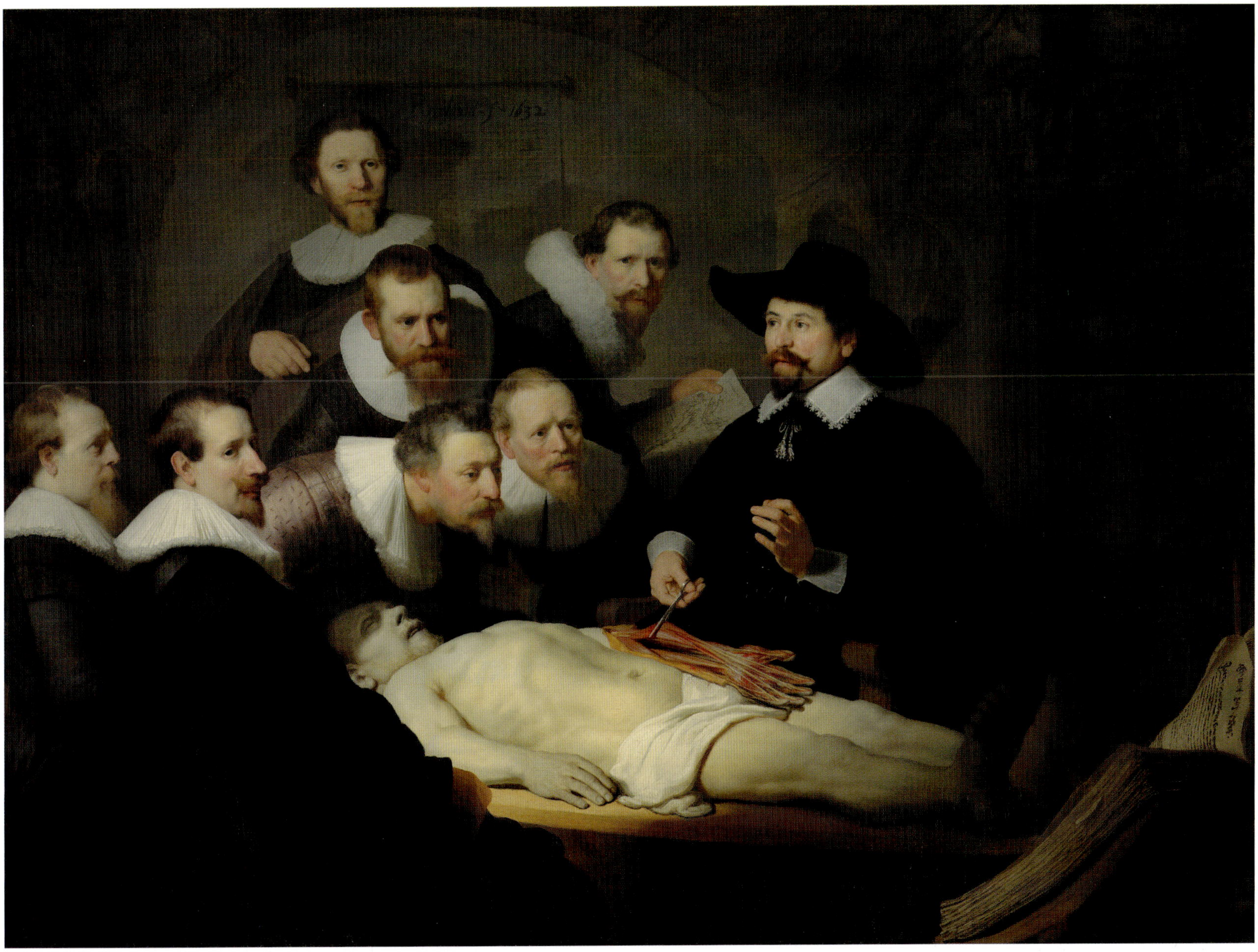

Some of the men gaze out of the picture, others appear to be looking at the book in the bottom right corner. Our eyes, though, are inevitably drawn to the corpse on the table. We know the dead man's name, Aris Kindt, and that he was hanged for armed robbery and theft of a coat. The lesson would have taken place on the day of his execution. We find this shocking today, but it was acceptable then. Perhaps, though, Rembrandt is asking us to consider not just a group of professionals and their work but also the value we place on human life.

Christ in the House of His Parents *or* The Carpenter's Shop

John Everett Millais
1849–50

This painting appears both very realistic and oddly strange. The scene takes place in a simple shed with people gathered around a carpentry worktable. There is another room behind with planks of wood lent against the wall, and through a doorway we see a field of sheep.

The painting has two titles; one religious, the other simply tells us where it takes place – a carpenter's shop. The figures look as if they have suddenly stopped their activity to focus on the young boy in the middle. He has cut his hand – perhaps on the nail poking out of the door being made behind him. A drop of blood has dripped onto his foot below.

The arrangement – or composition – of the figures is carefully balanced to form a kind of triangle shape with the young boy, who is Jesus Christ, and his mother, Mary, in the centre, his grandmother and father above, left and right. This arrangement was often used in the early religious paintings of the Italian Renaissance. The artists of this period hugely influenced the British artist Millais (1829–96) and others in England, who formed a group called the Pre-Raphaelite Brotherhood.

The painting is filled with Christian symbolism that tells us this is not any old carpenter's workshop. The wood, nails, Christ's wounded palm and the drop of blood on his foot are symbols of his crucifixion. The boy on the right bringing water to wash Christ's wound is a young John the Baptist. The dove on the ladder is a reference to the Holy Spirit. Next to this on the wall, the carpenter's triangle symbolises the Holy Trinity. The curious sheep are a reference to Christ, the good shepherd who cares for and protects people (his flock).

TAKE A LOOK AT Millais's painting *Mariana* (1851) to see further the extraordinary attention to detail found in his work.

FIND works by some of the Renaissance artists the Pre-Raphaelites admired in this book. Look for Leonardo da Vinci, Giovanni Bellini and Paolo Uccello.

When Millais first exhibited this painting, many people thought it was incredibly insulting to show Christ and the Holy Family as lowly, poorly-dressed people without shoes and standing on the dirt and sawdust floor. But for Millais, it was important to paint his subject as truthfully as possible and present Jesus's family as poor, honest and hard working.

Take Two Views of Women at Work

In both these paintings women are at work outdoors. They are similarly dressed in comfortable clothes that protect them from the weather. Painted around 50 years apart, both pictures were made at a time when much of the world's population still lived in the countryside and worked on the land. Most were poor peasants.

The Gleaners
Jean-François Millet
1857

In this painting by Frenchman Millet (1814–75), three peasant women are stooping to pick over (or glean) the ground for wheat grains that have been left behind after harvesting. It is too little for the farmer to bother with, but if you are poor you make sure that nothing is wasted. The painting is large - over a metre wide - a size, at that time, usually reserved for paintings of religious subjects, royalty or great myths and legends.

Two of the women are bent over at their work; their large hands indicate a life of manual labour. On the right one woman straightens up. She has tied her apron to create a large pocket for collecting the precious grain. *What words would you use to describe the work the women are doing?*

In the background, labourers gather the abundant crop into large haystacks. A figure on horseback surveys the scene - no doubt to keep an eye on things to make sure the labourers keep hard at work. *Why do you think the artist chose this backdrop for the gleaning women?*

Millet depicts his gleaners realistically in beautiful detail. He wanted to give them nobility. When this painting was first exhibited in Paris, many who saw it - who were mostly very well-off - were critical of its direct depiction of poverty. *Why do you think they felt this way? What do you think the artist wanted to say about the lives of these women?*

The artists look at these hard working peasant women in very contrasting ways. They have done this by using different colours, painting styles and details. But these pictures have also been influenced by strong political ideas about what it meant to be a farm labourer at that time.

Gardening
Natalia Goncharova
1908

This painting of Russian peasant women by Goncharova (1881–1962) feels entirely different. The large, bold brushstrokes have none of Millet's delicacy and realism. Her painting style reminds us of Braque and Picasso's Cubism (look in Still Lifes and History), and also Kandinsky and Marc (look in Landscapes and Animals), who were members of the Blue Rider group. She knew these artists' work and exhibited with them at the time.

Goncharova wanted to celebrate her country's traditional folk art as a way of showing support for the workers. The shape of the women's bodies are simple, their bare feet are large. Her images have a roughness similar to untrained, naïve artists. *Why do you think she chose to work in this way?*

There are echoes of Russia's traditional religious paintings of saints, called icons. We see this in the decorative patterns in the women's clothes where they drape around the knees and arms. Their faces are calm. *What words would you use to describe these women at work?*

Goncharova, educated and well-off, described her time spent in the countryside amongst peasants as 'joyful'. Her peasants are growing flowers rather than picking over the harvest leftovers for their survival. *What do you think the artist wanted to say about the lives of these women? How do her ideas compare with Millet's?*

The Making of a Fresco Showing the Building of a City

Diego Rivera
1931

The Mexican artist Diego Rivera (1886–1957) passionately believed that the creative work of artists is as important to our daily lives as other kinds of labour from construction work to medical care. So when he was commissioned to create a mural for an art school in San Francisco in the United States, he decided to express this idea by making two artworks in one – a painting inside a painting!

The wood scaffolding against the wall looks like you could climb onto it, but in fact it has been painted. This kind of optical illusion is called *trompe l'oeil*, French for 'trick of the eye'. On the scaffold a number of men are busy painting a scene with tall buildings and a large central figure. But when you look closer, there is a lot of confusion about who is painting and who is being painted!

In the centre, three of the five figures wear the same clothes – it's one person shown three times! The middle figure with legs dangling down is the artist with paintbrush and palette. His plump bottom protrudes just over the plank edge and into the room.

On the left, two of the three figures wear red jackets and blue trousers. Again, it's the same person twice! In between, a man with glasses and a checked shirt sculpts a stone head using a pneumatic drill. Another man works on the same statue below.

The men wearing suits looking at a large sheet of paper are architects and the head of the art association who commissioned this mural.

Lower right, a woman and two men stand around a table. The tools of their trade – drawing and measuring instruments – indicate their work as designers, architects and engineers.

Above are the construction workers, putting their designs into practice. All the construction workers wear blue overalls and a cap. So does the towering central figure being painted onto the wall – with his intense eyes and a solemn face. Rivera celebrates and honours all workers and their contribution to the building of our modern world.

TAKE A LOOK AT some public murals commissioned by the US government in the Federal Art Project. This scheme was set up to provide work for artists during the economic depression of the 1930s.

Hammering Man
Jonathan Borofsky
1990

The greatest works of art aren't always found in galleries, museums and other important buildings. There are wonderful artworks outside for everyone to enjoy known as public art. You can find commemorative statues in just about any park or square. They usually remember and celebrate someone famous or soldiers who have fought and died at war. But what about this monumental sculpture of a man? What can he possibly commemorate?

The Frankfurt Trade Fair buildings, in Germany, make up one of the largest exhibition venues in the world. Businesses come here to showcase and sell their latest products at themed events, from books to airplanes. When American artist Borofsky (1942–) was commissioned to make a sculpture to be placed outside the Trade Fair's new building, he decided to commemorate the unsung heroes whose hard work is behind a trade fair.

Hammering Man at Frankfurt is a symbol of the workers of the world (a bit like Diego Rivera's giant worker painted in his mural). He stands 21 metres tall – around the height of a six-storey building – and each foot is nearly the size of a car! He is made of a thick sheet of strong steel and is painted black so he makes a very striking silhouette against the sky.

Head bent over his task, this is a kinetic sculpture, meaning that it moves. You can see the motor in his shoulder, which powers the arm that holds the hammer to move slowly and continuously up and down – forever hammering day and night, year in and year out.

TAKE A LOOK AT the amazing kinetic sculptures of Jean Tinguely (1925–91) that have mechanical moving parts that turn, crank, rotate and sometimes lift off! What do these tell us about our daily lives of work?

This was such a popular public sculpture that Borofsky was invited to install his *Hammering Man* in other locations around the world, mostly in large cities, but also in parks created especially to exhibit sculptures. The *Hammering Man* in Seoul, Korea is taller at 22 metres. Other places it is found include Los Angeles and Seattle, in the United States, Basel, Switzerland, and Lillestrøm, Norway. The artist says that he wanted to create a worldwide sculpture about work that connects us all together.

Chicago, Board of Trade II
Andreas Gursky
1999

We end our gallery looking at the world of work with a picture of frenetic activity! The artist has created this image by taking several photographs of his subject and then skilfully merging them using a computer so that they appear to be one.

The Chicago Board of Trade is a kind of virtual marketplace where people make money by trading in the future supplies of commodities from wheat, butter and soybeans to gold and silver. These are bought and sold by hundreds of traders every day. The prices go up and down all of the time, and the traders need to know when to buy or sell. The important thing is not to lose money!

The main trading takes place in the round area with the green floor, called the 'pit'. Different coloured jackets are worn to help traders identify who they are doing business with. The pit is filled with people shouting and waving their arms to attract the person they want to trade with. Some of the figures here are blurred, or appear more than once, giving the sense of movement – a hive of activity!

German artist Gursky (1955–) has chosen to create his picture from a high viewpoint. From a distance all the individual people have become a bustling mass or swarm. What an incredible, chaotic mass of colour and commotion! It looks almost like an abstract painting. The artist is very interested in how we live in the modern world today, how each and everyone's separate lives are just one part of a huge global economy that we find hard to understand.

At the beginning of this gallery we saw a moneylender weighing and deciding the value of jewels and gold for the purposes of trade. Gursky's picture presents us with the same general principle, but this trading is taking place 400 years later, based around 'futures', something that does not even exist yet. The world economy has grown enormously and money is now at the centre of all of our lives in a different way.

TAKE A LOOK AT the photographic collages of David Hockney (1937–). He has also combined multiple photographs or digital images to create pictures, for example, *Still Life Blue Guitar 4th April 1982* (1982) or *Pearblossom Highway* (1986).

FIND Njikeka Akunyili Crosby in the Still Lifes gallery. She also uses photography in her work. How does her technique vary from Gursky's?

Play

Do you enjoy playing indoors on a computer, or do you prefer to play games or team sports outdoors? Or do you just like to meet up and chat with your friends? Play can take many forms. It is our leisure time: what we do when we relax or have time off.

Perhaps your parents or grandparents have told you about how they used to play when they were growing up? Their childhood games and toys were probably quite different from yours, but has *how* humans play changed that much over time? In this final gallery, let's take a look at how artists depict people – young and old – relaxing, exercising and playing.

The Jockey of Artemision

artist unknown

around 150–140BCE

This powerful bronze sculpture of a boy riding a horse was made over 2,000 years ago in Greece. The Olympics that we know today had their beginnings in ancient Greece, and at that time horse racing was one of the most popular and important of all the sports.

This horse and jockey are bigger than life-size and incredibly lifelike. They are captured at an exhilarating moment as they strain to get to the finishing line. The horse's front legs are raised in the air, mid-gallop at full speed, with eyes wide, ears flattened, nostrils widened and mouth open.

The boy is young, thought to be just ten years old, and looks very small compared to the horse. In his left hand are the remains of what would have been the horse's reins. His expression isn't one of triumph, but of anticipation as he looks over his left shoulder. Perhaps he is checking to see if anyone is about to overtake him. His mouth is slightly open with concentration and exhaustion as he leans into the neck of the horse to keep his balance. Do you think this is play for him?

The sculptor has closely studied the details for both figures. Can you see the horse's muscles and the strained veins? The boy's short tunic is tied at the waist and flows in the wind, showing his strong arms and legs. If you look at his facial features, can you tell what his heritage is? It is thought he may have been from Africa, as Greece had many links with North Africa at the time.

FIND Stubbs' picture of a horse being attacked by a lion in the Animals gallery. How have both artists used the anatomical detail of the horse to add drama to their work?

One Hundred Children in the Long Spring

Su Hanchen

mid-12th century CE

Around 900 years ago, during the Song Dynasty (960–1279) in China, a fashion developed for paintings of children at play. These were popular because children were considered to be 'auspicious' – a sign of future success – so paintings of them brought good luck. Chinese artist Su Hanchen (working c.1130–70) was particularly admired for his depiction of children.

Su Hanchen painted this long scroll of one hundred boys in a spring garden. This number of children brings a lot of good luck! He shows all sorts of playful action, from kicking a ball to board games. In the section we have focused on, some boys are engrossed in looking at a scroll painting themselves – just like you are in this book!

The children are surrounded by nature, but their attention is on the scroll, which depicts a bamboo plant. Are they learning about the bamboo forest behind them? One child invites an older friend or teacher, who carries a hawk, to have a look.

Another lifts his hand delicately over the scroll, as though he wants to touch but knows he shouldn't, whilst his friend peeks over his shoulder. His eyes, directed towards the picture, show the same seriousness and intense concentration as the others. They seem almost like small adults.

But the two younger boys at the front of the picture are not interested in the scroll. One is having fun with some twigs he has found. The other, in a multicoloured jacket, wants to play too. Hanchen has carefully picked out the detail in the children's clothing and hairstyles. These seem to echo the elegance of their natural surroundings.

TAKE A LOOK AT Pieter Breugel the Elder's *Children's Games* (1560), which shows a world of children all at different kinds of play – serious, silly, rough and gentle – just like all of life!

But all this detail does not detract from the focus of the work – the way children play. Whilst we are looking at children from a long time ago, their total absorption in their activities is instantly recognisable today. It was Hanchen's ability to capture this quality that made his work so popular.

The Chess Game
Sofonisba Anguissola
1555

Here is a calm and happy depiction of play. Three young girls are grouped around a chessboard. The two older ones are playing the game and an older woman looks on. Chess is one of the oldest board games. It was invented in India around 1,500 years ago.

The Italian artist Sofonisba Anguissola (c.1532–1625) was only 20 when she painted this beautiful work. Can you see the words along the edge of the chessboard? She has written us a note in Latin, which translates as: 'Sofonisba Anguissola virgin daughter of Amilcare painted these three sisters and a maid from life.'

We know the sisters' names: Luca is on the left and looks directly at us as she moves a chess piece with her right hand. Her opponent, Minerva, looks at her older sister with right hand raised and seems to be saying, 'You've got me!' The youngest sister, Europa, watches and laughs as the game unfolds.

Can you tell what kind of lifestyle they had? Look at their gold embroidered clothes, their necklaces and the jewellery in their elaborate hairstyles. How do they compare to the garments worn by the older woman? The chessboard is on a beautifully patterned rug. They're outside, perhaps in a garden. The leaves of an oak tree on the left symbolise strong family relationships. What can you see in the far distance?

At the time in Europe, women were allowed to play chess as it was considered to be an educational exercise, based on skill. They were forbidden to play games of luck, such as cards or dice. People also disapproved of women becoming artists. Anguissola is a rare exception because of her wealth. Even so, she was limited to the subjects that she was allowed to paint, so she naturally chose people in her own family. As well as a group portrait of her sisters and their maid, this is also a tender picture of sibling rivalry and love.

FIND the double portrait of twin sisters by Alice Neel in the Portraits gallery. Compare how the two artists depict love and care between siblings.

Winter Landscape with Ice Skaters

Hendrick Avercamp
1608

This wonderful wintry scene is buzzing with activity! We have a bird's eye view – as if we're sitting atop a tall tree like the ones in the picture, with their bare branches spreading out against the sky. You can almost feel the bitter cold, but the whole town seems to be outdoors having fun on the ice. Well, most people anyway ...

This is one of many such landscapes that Dutch artist Hendrick Avercamp (1585–1634) made during a period of unusually cold winters, known as the Little Ice Age. The flat land and waterways, which Holland is famous for, remained frozen for many months and people adapted to getting about on the ice. Like other artists of the time, Avercamp wanted to explore everyday life and the sensations people experienced in the outdoors.

The incredible, closely observed detail in this large painting tells us a lot about life 400 years ago. Look for birds, dogs, barrels and boats. There are even bits of graffiti, including the artist's name! The main red brick building has a coat of arms, a crescent moon sign and other features that tell us it is a brewery. Behind it is a grey stone church, looking gloomy and neglected when compared to the bustle everywhere else.

But it is the people who are the most fascinating. There are as many as 250 figures of all ages and from all walks of life in this picture. In the far distance some are depicted with just a tiny brushstroke. There are gentlemen playing a game of kolf (a game resembling ice hockey); a man carrying heavy baskets being greeted by a child; a lavishly dressed group approached by a beggar in tattered clothes ... What other stories can you find?

FIND two other icy pictures in the Landscapes gallery. How does the way Avercamp uses colour to create a sense of the cold and looking into the far distance compare with these?

We know that the artist was deaf and did not speak, which some say gave him the ability to give us this sense of playful joy, focusing on the visual variety of the world around him. The pleasure that people get from looking at this action-packed painting made Avercamp one of the most celebrated and popular artists of his day. This is a masterpiece from a period in Dutch art which is known as the Golden Age of Painting. It was a time when Dutch artists, such as Avercamp, developed a detailed, realistic style which focused on everyday life.

The Straw Manikin
Francisco de Goya
1791–92

What a most curious sight! What are these four young women up to? They are clearly having fun, but there's definitely something very unusual about the figure that they have launched into the sky!

This painting is one of around 60 created by Spanish artist Francisco de Goya (1746–1828) for King Carlos IV of Spain. The images were made into large tapestries to be hung in the king's palace. The scenes show adults and children in the countryside playing games, eating, dancing and generally having fun!

In our painting each woman holds a section of the cloth from which the figure has been thrown. They are gaily dressed in the fashion of the time – full skirts with plenty of lace, pretty headdresses and buckled shoes.

In contrast, the arms and legs of the figure being tossed are limp. Its unsmiling face is a mask with painted lips and staring eyes, like a doll or a puppet. The artist has really drawn our attention by placing this figure in the centre of the painting, as if hanging in the air against white clouds and blue sky.

It is, in fact, a life-size doll, or manikin, that is filled with straw. The game of blanket-tossing was popular at Spanish carnivals and it was usually something that young men performed on a friend who was about to be married. So why does this artist swap the men with young women and a manikin?

Goya is well known for a particular kind of humour in his art called satire. This is when humour is used to show you something about someone or something that may be true, but not necessarily funny or even perhaps a bit cruel. If you look carefully again, maybe you'll think that underneath the fun and playfulness there is something a little sinister. Perhaps Goya is telling us that strong-minded women can have power over weak men!

TAKE A LOOK AT
Goya's print
The Sleep of Reason Produces Monsters,
from his *Los Caprichos* series.
Goya sometimes explored dreams and nightmares in his work.

FIND
Dorothea Tanning's doll-like figure in her painting in the Storytelling gallery. How is her figure different from Goya's?

Carnation, Lily, Lily, Rose

John Singer Sargent

1885–86

Two sisters stand in a garden of beautiful white flowers and dark green foliage. Dolly (left) is eleven and Polly (right) is seven. They seem completely absorbed in lighting Chinese paper lanterns using long wooden matches. How can you help but be drawn into the concentration on their faces and the almost magical glow of the orange and pink?

For many, this painting is pure tranquillity, and it is no surprise that it is one of the most loved artworks in the museum where it hangs. It is set at twilight – a fleeting moment at the end of the day when the setting sun can suddenly produce a burst of orange and everything seems miraculously illuminated.

American artist Sargent (1856–1925) was good friends with Claude Monet. Remember Monet's painting in the Landscapes gallery where the artist shows us the morning light, with the Sun rising? Both Monet's and this work are painted in an Impressionist style. However, whereas Monet created his painting very quickly, possibly in just one morning, Sargent took a very different approach.

Like the other Impressionists, it was important for Sargent to paint outdoors *en plein air* (French for in the open air), right in front of his subject matter. But Sargent's technique was not speedy and immediate. Twilight only lasts for around 20 minutes each day, so to capture this he worked on his masterpiece over several months during summer and autumn, spread over two years. Imagine how frustrating it must have been for the two girls to have to pose continually as the evening temperature dropped!

But this huge effort to capture the special light has certainly paid off for Sargent, whose great skill with a paintbrush is everywhere. See how the lamplight shines on Polly's face and hand, and how abstract splodges of paint suddenly come alive as glimmering light glowing through the dark green leaves. This painting is admired equally for the way in which it was painted as it is for the subject matter.

TAKE A LOOK AT the paintings of Georges de la Tour (1593-1652) to see how he uses candlelight to illuminate faces in a dramatic way.

Take Two Sunny Afternoons

Who doesn't love being outdoors on a sunny summer's afternoon? These paintings were made just over a hundred years apart – one in France and the other in the United States. Both are on a grand scale (over 3 metres wide), particularly the one on the right where the figures in the foreground have been painted roughly life-size.

A Sunday Afternoon on the Island of La Grande Jatte

Georges Seurat
1884-86

French artist Georges Seurat (1859–91) worked at a time when the Impressionists were painting with bold, hurried brushstrokes to capture their subjects. Leisure scenes like this one were popular. But Seurat developed a very different painting technique called pointillism, which he saw as more scientific. This is a method of applying thousands of tiny dots of paint in many different colours.

During the late 19th century, Sundays were the only day off from work. People would dress in their most fashionable clothes, and stroll around, or promenade, in parks purely for pleasure. *How are people showing off their 'Sunday best' in this painting?*

Each figure is carefully placed in the scene creating strong vertical lines and a balanced picture composition. Many are in profile as is often found in ancient Egyptian art. *What effect does this have on how you view the people?*

Look closely to see the tiny dots of colour Seurat has used. It is our eyes rather than the paintbrush that blend them together to make shapes. *How does Seurat's technique contribute towards the sense of calm and order in this painting?*

The artists have chosen similar subjects – people relaxing outdoors at the waterfront, socialising with friends and family on a sunny afternoon. Both paintings celebrate leisure time and the way city dwellers use parks and open spaces on their day off to walk around, people watch and maybe show off a little themselves.

Past Times

Kerry James Marshall 1997

African American artist Kerry James Marshall (1955–) likes to observe everyday life. He paints people in their homes, in cafés, on the street, at the hairdressers, or just relaxing. He loves, too, the 19th-century paintings of people at play, such as Seurat's famous masterpiece (which is in the art museum in Marshall's hometown of Chicago). But these works do not feature African Americans. Marshall wants to change this.

There are plenty of leisure activities in this picture, from golfing to water-skiing. Lyrics of songs flow from the radios: 'It was just my imagination …' and 'Got my mind on my money …' *What are these details saying about the people in this painting?*

This waterside scene shows a family picnicking. The father plays golf and a young girl croquet. A speedboat darts about. These leisure activities are normally associated with prosperous, white middle-class lifestyles. A boy listens to a radio while his mother unpacks the picnic basket. The mother and her two children look straight out at us, the viewer. *What effect does their direct gaze have?*

The tower blocks on the horizon are where many of the black community in Chicago live. The banner stretching across the background reads, 'Who plays … all of the heart and … skill / Will also work with heart and will.' *How does this message contribute towards a sense of celebration in this picture?*

Gallery Matrix

Here is a visual guide to the eight galleries of this book.

Portraits

Cave of the Hands

Portrait of Terentius Neo and His Wife

Armada Portrait of Queen Elizabeth I

Barack Obama

Las Meninas

Self Portrait in a Straw Hat

Portrait Head of John Henry

The De Vegh Twins

Landscapes

Landscape with Charon Crossing the Styx

Wanderer above the Sea of Fog

Snow Storm: Hannibal and His Army Crossing the Alps

Ejiri in Suruga Province

Impression, Sunrise

Composition IV

Black Mesa Landscape

Ntange Dreaming

Storytelling

Painted panel of Tatiaset

St Francis in Ecstasy

Landscape with the Fall of Icarus

Searching the Mountains for Demons

Illustration from the Mewar Ramayana

Carnival of Harlequin

Eine Kleine Nachtmusik

The Annunciation of the Virgin Deal

History

Napoleon Crossing the Alps

The Bayeux Tapestry

The Battle of San Romano

Babur Receives a Courtier

The Last of England

Guernica

The Sunflower Quilting Bee at Arles

Throne of Weapons

It also gives you suggestions for how you could mix up the galleries and put many of these masterpieces somewhere else altogether.

Animals

Cats, Lions and a Dragon

Hippopotamus

Rhinoceros

Spectacled Caiman with South American False Coral Snake

Lion Attacking a Horse

Tiger Family and Magpies

Noah's Ark

The Yellow Cow

Still Lifes

Still Life with Flowers and Fruit

The Ray

The Black Marble Clock

Sunflowers

Still Life: Le Jour

Red Interior, Still Life on a Blue Table

Still Life with Crystal Bowl

Grandmother's Parlour

Work

The Moneylender and His Wife

The Anatomy Lesson of Dr Nicolaes Tulp

Christ in the House of His Parents (The Carpenter's Shop)

The Gleaners

Gardening

The Making of a Fresco Showing the Building of a City

Hammering Man

Chicago, Board of Trade II

Play

The Jockey of Artemision

One Hundred Children in the Long Spring

The Chess Game

Winter Landscape with Ice Skaters

The Straw Manikin

Carnation, Lily, Lily, Rose

A Sunday Afternoon on the Island of La Grand Jatte

Past Times

Finishing Pieces

To finish off, here is a packed gallery for you to try out your new skills of looking at great works of art. With the help of the Gallery Matrix, choose where in the book you would put each artwork – perhaps some might need a whole new gallery. There are a few ideas and questions to guide you, but from now on it's up to you!

Spoonbridge and Cherry, 1988, Claes Oldenburg and Coosje van Bruggen
Did you know that Pop Art stands for 'popular'? Pop artists often use everyday objects in ways that you wouldn't expect. Here they also play around with scale and function.

Still Life with Bowl of Citrons, late 1640s, Giovanna Garzoni
This artist is celebrated for her skill in painting still lifes in a very naturalistic way and with great accuracy. Look for the wasp that has just landed on the lemon.

Landscape with Calligraphy, 1555-1636 exact date unknown, Dong Qichang
Chinese landscape painting traditionally often combines images with writing, or calligraphy. How do the pictures in the Landscape gallery compare to this?

A Bar at the Follies Bergère, 1882, Édouard Manet
Who is the woman looking at? Who is the man in the top hat talking to? Is the scene behind just a reflection? Where else have we seen a crystal bowl of fruit?

View of Toledo, 1599-1600, El Greco
A city perches on hills behind intense green fields underneath a stormy looking sky. How does this city compare with other cities we have seen in this book?

The Ambassadors, 1533, Hans Holbein the Younger
Two men look straight out at us from luxurious surroundings. Globes, measuring and musical instruments and books are on the table. What do these tell us about who they are? What is the strange distorted object in the foreground?

Millicent Garrett Fawcett, 2018, Gillian Wearing
Millicent Fawcett fought for women's right to vote. This statue stands as the only woman alongside statues of male politicians in Parliament Square, London. What other artists in this book use art to express human rights?

Baku: Monster that Eats Nightmares, 18th century, Gechū
This amazing monster is only 9.5 cm high. This type of miniature Japanese sculpture is called Netsuke. Where else in this book can you find such fantastical creatures?

The Scream, 1893, Edvard Munch
The swirling blue water, red sky and angle of the bridge railing create drama. The figure in front holds his hands to his skull-like head. How do other artists show emotion?

Nocturne: Blue and Gold – Old Battersea Bridge, 1872–75, James Abbott McNeill Whistler
A nocturne is a kind of melodic music, but it also means night. The gold lights from the houses are reflected in the water, but what are the gold specks in the sky?

The Hay Wain, 1821, John Constable
This artist is best known for his pictures of the countryside and his outstanding ability to paint clouds. Look back to compare his work with other artists interested in these features.

Pietà, 1498–99, Michelangelo
Christ lies dead across his mother's lap. Carved from marble, this sculpture was created for Christians to remember Christ's sacrifice for humanity. Look back to find other works about religious or spiritual belief.

The Kiss, 1907–08, Gustav Klimt
The artist uses a luscious gold background and wonderful patterns. How is this appropriate for the moment depicted in the painting?

The Milkmaid, c.1660, Johannes Vermeer
In this beautiful, highly realistic painting, the simple act of pouring milk from a pitcher has an otherworldly quality. Can you remember the term to describe the angled light?

Red Cavalry Riding, 1928–32, Kazimir Malevich
At first this looks like an abstract painting with strips of colour, but then you see soldiers on horseback dashing across the horizon. Would you put this in the History or Landscapes gallery? Or could it go in the Animals gallery?

The Sorrow of Telemachus, 1783, Angelica Kauffman
The title of this painting tells us that it is sorrowful. It is also full of drama. How has Kaufman shown us this? Which figure do you think is Telemachus?

Arearea, 1892, Paul Gauguin
This scene of women and a dog was painted in Tahiti. Its bold areas of colour and simple stylised forms are similar to one of the artists in the Animals gallery. Can you find which one?

Terracotta Army of Qin Shin Huang, Emperor of China, 210–209BCE, artists unknown
Here are some of the 8,000 ceramic soldiers buried over 2,000 years ago to protect the Chinese emperor in the afterlife. Find the Egyptian object also created for its protective powers.

The Cradle, 1872, Berthe Morisot
Morisot has used a limited range of colours to show us an intimate scene of motherly love. Look back to find other artists whose works feature tender family scenes.

Benin Bronze, 18th century, **artist unknown**
This African sculpture is cast from bronze, achieving wonderful detail. Can you find another work where the artist uses bronze to make the forms come to life?

Portrait of the Artist's Wife, 1918, **Amedeo Modigliani**
A contemporary of the Cubists, Modigliani was also interested in African sculpture. You can see both these influences in the simplified shapes of this figure.

Yellow Pumpkin, 1994, Yayoi Kusama
This artist has painted dots since childhood and the pumpkin is one of her favourite objects. For her it conveys generosity and spirituality. What artist uses the sunflower as a symbol of gratitude?

Judith and her Maidservant with the Head of Holofernes, 1623–25, Artemisia Gentileschi
Both women look out of the picture towards a source of strong light, which captures the drama. What other artists in the book use light in a similar way?

The Arnolfini Portrait, 1434, Jan van Eyck
After nearly 600 years this painting still fascinates us. It is a double portrait to mark the couple's marriage. There are many clues to tell us who they are. What ones can you find? What other double portraits can you find in this book?

Maman, 1999, Louise Bourgeois
This artist's work often expresses her feminist beliefs. 'Maman' means mother in French. and is shown here as a colossal female spider. How friendly does she look to you?

Useful Art Words

Abstraction describes art made up of colours and shapes - whether geometrical or organic - that do not represent anything other than itself. Artworks made in this way are said to be **abstract**.

Acrylic paint is made from *pigments* held in a type of liquid plastic. It can be mixed with water for different effects but dries very quickly after use and becomes water resistant.

Anatomy is the study of structures of living things, including the human body and animals.

Attribution is the activity of stating a work has been made by a particular artist. When a painting is unsigned or made in a way very similar to another artist, its attribution may be an area for discussion.

The **Blue Rider** was a group of German and Russian artists that came together between 1911 and 1914. They believed in expressing their emotions spontaneously through their art, the connection between visual art and music, and that colour could suggest spirituality.

Bronze is a metal alloy made mostly of copper and tin that is used in sculpture because it is easy to melt and *cast*. It is also liked for its rich, varied colour.

A **bust** is a sculpture of a person's head, often also including shoulders and chest.

Canvas is a type of cloth made from hemp or flax. Typically stretched on a frame and often treated, it can be used as a surface to paint on in *oil* or *acrylic paint*.

To **cast** is to make a sculpture from pouring melted or molten metal into a shaped container or 'mould'. The metal becomes hard as it cools, taking the shape of the container.

Chiaroscuro is an Italian word (meaning 'light-dark') used to describe how painters show solid form through the representation of strong contrasts of light and darkness.

A **cityscape** is a *landscape* of an urban or city area.

A **collage** is an artwork made from different found or gathered materials, which could include, fabric, paper, plastic, or even fragments of other artworks, all glued together to form a new image. The word describes the process and also the finished result.

To **commission** an artist is to employ them to create a specific artwork.

The **composition** of an artwork is the arrangement of the different parts in a painting or sculpture that encourage the eye to move around the work. Its aim is to please the eye while revealing the subject and meaning of the work to the viewer.

Cubism is an art movement dating from the early 20th century which uses geometric shapes to create images of subjects as if they were seen from many different angles at the same time.

An **easel** is the frame that holds a *canvas* or other surface in place as an artist paints or draws on it.

Flemish describes the art and artists that came from what is now known as Belgium and its neighbouring areas from the 15th to 17th centuries.

Fresco is a type of wall painting where the paint is applied directly to wet plastered walls.

A **glaze** is a glass coating placed on clay or ceramic to decorate or waterproof it. The coating is applied wet and then fused to the clay through heating to extremely high temperatures in a kiln.

The **Harlem Renaissance** was an art movement based in Harlem, an area of Manhattan, New York, in the 1920s and 1930s. It looked to revive and celebrate African American culture and heritage, including its art, music and literature, in a similar way as the earlier European *Renaissance* rediscovered its Roman and Greek heritage. Its influence was of great global significance.

A **horizon line** is the furthest line you can see in the distance, where the Earth seems to touch the sky.

Impasto is a word used to describe paint that has been applied very thickly, often so you can see its texture.

The **Impressionists** were a group of French artists who exhibited together between 1874 and 1886. They particularly aimed to depict the changing quality of light, often working outside and in a style that broke many of the rules of art at the time but became very influential. It is often described as **Impressionism**.

The word **landscape** describes the land, sea and sky and the physical features within it. A landscape painting is one where this is its principal or strong focus of interest.

Medieval, or the Middle Ages, is the period in European history roughly between 600 to 1500 that lies between the fall of the Roman Empire and the emergence of the *Renaissance* era.

Memento mori is a Latin phrase meaning 'remember you must die', describing objects, or a picture that contains these objects, that symbolise the fact that human life ends in death. These objects can include skulls, clocks, and withering flowers.

A **miniature** is a very small work of art, often a *portrait*, containing extraordinary detail despite its size.

A **mural** is a large painting made on a wall of a building or room.

Naïve is a way of describing artists (and their art) who have received no formal training or education in making art so may not fully understand techniques in areas such as *anatomy* or *perspective*.

Neoclassicism was a cultural movement, particularly linked to art and architecture, that began in Europe in the middle of the 18th century that drew its inspiration from ancient Greece and Rome.

Oil paint is the material most often used for painting pictures on *canvas*. The *pigments* are held in an oil which gradually dries out to form a tough layer of paint on the surface it is applied to. The oldest oil paintings known date from 650CE in Bamiyan, Afghanistan, but became popular during the *Renaissance*.

A **palette** is a flat surface that artists use to hold and mix paints as they work; it is often made of wood and can be held in the hand. The word palette can also be used to describe the range of colours an artist uses.

In art, **perspective** is the technique used so that objects represented in two dimensions can appear to exist in a three-dimensional space where objects closer to the viewer appear larger than those further away.

Pigments are colours that can be dried into powders and mixed with liquids to form paint - they can be natural or manufactured.

En plein air is French for 'in the open air'. It is the term used to describe paintings that have been made entirely outside in front of the subject.

Pointillism is a scientific approach to painting developed in the late 19th century from *Impressionism*, where pictures are created from thousands of dots of pure colour which the eye mixes together.

Pop art is an attitude to making art that came to prominence internationally in the early 1960s. It uses popular culture - found in images such as advertising and comic strips - in its creation or subject matter.

A **portrait** is a representational record of a particular person.

A **power portrait** is a *portrait* that has usually been *commissioned* of a person who is in a position of power such as a monarch or president. Some such portraits enhance and communicate that sense of power as a form of propaganda.

The **Pre-Raphaelite Brotherhood** was a group of 19th century British artists that aimed to treat serious subjects in a highly realistic and natural way, yet also using an elaborate system of *symbols*. They admired the work of *medieval* and early *Renaissance* artists who came before the artist Raphael (1483-1520).

Public art is art that is on display for anyone to see in public places (rather than a museum or gallery). It can include statues in the park but also performances on the street.

Renaissance meaning rebirth, is the period in European art history when people rediscovered the art and learning of ancient Greece and Rome. It began around 1400 in Italy reaching its height there around at the start of the 16th century, but its ideas spread all around Europe.

Romanticism describes a European movement in art and literature that began in the second half of the 18th century and was extremely influential in the 19th century. It was fascinated by both personal feelings and the natural world.

A **seascape** is a *landscape* where the sea is the dominant feature.

A **self-portrait** is a *portrait* of an artist made by that artist. Often, they depict the artist at work or are more personal expressions of emotions or psychology. Some artists have used the self-portrait as a kind of publicity.

A **silhouette** is the dark shape or outline created by something or someone against a brighter background. This often takes the form of a *portrait* in profile.

A **sketch** is a rough drawing or painting made by an artist often as a study in preparation for an artwork.

A **stencil** is a shape used to create an image by applying colour around or through it to a surface beneath it.

A **still life** is a work whose main subject matter is made up of things that do not move, often featuring everyday objects, flowers and fruit.

A **street artist** is an artist who makes art unofficially in public places that can be seen by anyone. Someone who spray-paints graffiti is a street artist, for example.

The **sublime** is a type of art from the 18th and 19th centuries linked to *Romanticism*. It is designed to provoke or is inspired by very strong emotions, such as fear or awe, particularly in relation to the natural world.

Surrealism was a 20th-century movement in art and literature. It was inspired by the way the mind worked, making connections and creating other realities, often unconsciously and in dreams.

A **symbol** is something used to represent ideas, qualities or emotions - for instance, an owl may be depicted to symbolise intelligence, the use of the colour red could symbolise passion and excitement.

A **tapestry** is an expanse of fabric which has either had a pictorial image or decorative design woven into it or embroidered on to it using different colour threads.

Trompe l'oeil is the French for 'deceives the eye'. It describes a painting that tricks the viewer into thinking they are looking at a real object when in fact it is just a painting.

The **vanishing point** is a term used in the art technique of *perspective*. It describes the point, furthest from the viewer, where lines that are actually parallel (railway tracks, for instance) appear instead to come together and meet if they are continued towards the *horizon line*.

Woodblock printing is a method of printing where an image is carved from a block of wood so it stands out in relief. This image is then covered in paint or ink and printed on to another surface - often a sheet of paper.

Index

Aboriginal Peoples 32-33
abstract art 18, 29, 32, 102, 114, 123
acrylic paint 32
Africa / African 88, 105, 124
African American 16, 86, 117
afterlife 20, 36, 62, 124
Akunyili Crosby, Njideka 60-61, 103
America / American 10, 11, 16, 18, 32, 44, 59, 73, 82, 86-87, 100, 114, 117
anatomy 34-35, 40, 92-93, 105
Anguissola, Sofonisba 39, 108-109
animals 21, 30, 32, 34-47, 64, 69, 84, 104-105
Argentina 6
armies 23, 76-77, 78-79, 124
art school 14, 16, 40, 86, 98
Australia / Australian 32-33, 82
Avercamp, Hendrick 110-111

battles 10, 23, 76, 78-79, 80
Beg, Farrukh 71, 80-81
Bellini, Giovanni 64-65
birds 21, 42, 44, 110
Blue Rider, the 28, 46-47, 97
boats 20, 26, 36, 44, 66, 82, 110
books 38, 40, 59, 64, 80-81, 90, 93, 100, 106, 121
Borofsky, Jonathan 100-101
Bourgeois, Louise 125
boys 66, 94, 104-105, 106, 117
Braque, Georges 56-57, 97
bronze 16, 104, 124
Brown, Ford Maddox 82-83
Bruegel, Pieter the Elder 66-67
van Bruggen, Coosje 120
buildings 20, 26, 98, 100, 110
Bunchō, Tani 42-43

Caravaggio, Michelangelo di 48-49, 50, 56
cats 34-35, 42, 51
cave paintings 6-7
Cézanne, Paul 31, 52-53
Chardin, Jean-Baptiste 50-51
children 6, 18, 74, 82, 84, 106-107, 110, 112, 117
China / Chinese 42, 68-69, 106, 120, 124
Christians / Christianity 44, 49, 64, 94, 122
cities 8, 18, 21, 46, 66, 82, 84, 90, 98, 101, 117, 121
clothes 8, 10, 14, 96-97, 98, 106, 108, 110, 116
clouds 22-23, 26, 44, 64, 76, 112, 122
coastlines 20, 66
comics 59, 69, 70, 78
commissions 8-9, 40, 70, 76, 77, 78, 79, 81, 92, 98, 100
computers 74-75, 102
Constable, John 122
construction 98-99
countryside 20, 46, 97, 112, 122
Cubism 56-57, 84, 97, 124

David, Jacques-Louis 76-77
death 36, 50, 66-67
Din, Sahib 70-71
drawings 34, 37, 38-39, 40, 75, 98
Dürer, Albrecht 25, 37
Dutch / Holland 14, 21, 54, 92, 110-111

Egypt / Egyptians 36, 62-63, 116
El Greco 121
England / English 10, 22, 40, 78, 82, 94
Europe 32, 37, 39, 42, 76, 86, 109
van Eyck, Jan 75, 91, 125

Fairey, Shepard 11
families 6, 18, 42, 82, 95, 108-109, 117
farming 96
fashion 8, 112
fields 20, 64, 86, 94, 121
fish 50-51
Flemish 20, 90-91
flowers 30, 36, 38, 48, 54, 58, 62, 63, 75, 80, 85, 86, 97, 114
forests 20, 106
France / French 14, 16, 45, 50, 54, 56, 76, 78, 86, 116
frescoes 8, 98
Friedrich, Caspar David 22, 23
fruit 48-49, 58, 59

games 8, 104, 106, 108-109, 110, 112
gardens 20, 58, 60, 71, 97, 106, 108, 114
Garzoni, Giovanna 120
Gauguin, Paul 54, 124
Gechū 122
Gentileschi, Artemisia 125
Germany / German 22, 37, 38, 46, 84, 100, 102
girls 12, 18, 73, 82, 108, 114, 117
gods 10, 44, 62-63, 64-65, 68
van Gogh, Vincent 54-55, 73, 86
Goncharova, Natalia 97
Goya, Francisco de 85, 112-113
Greeks / Greece 16, 65, 66, 76, 104-105
group portraits 12, 92, 109
Gursky, Andreas 102-103

Hanchen, Su 106-107
hands 6-7, 10, 14, 18, 58, 62, 82, 90, 92, 94, 96, 105, 106, 108, 114, 122
heaven 20-21, 65, 66
hell 20-21
Hicks, Edward 44-45
hills 28, 30, 64, 70
history 23, 74, 76-89
Hokusai, Katsushika 24-25, 26
Holbein, Hans the Younger 121
horses 28, 40-41, 44, 66, 76, 78, 84, 104-105

illustration 59, 70, 71, 75, 80-81
Impressionism / Impressionists 27, 53, 114, 116
India / Indian 37, 70, 80, 108
Italy / Italian 23, 34, 48, 64-65, 76, 79, 94, 108

Japan / Japanese 24-25, 42, 122

Kandinsky, Wassily 28-29, 46, 97
Kauffman, Angelica 15, 123
kinetic sculptures 100-101
kings 10, 12, 37, 77, 78, 112
Klimt, Gustav 123
Kngwarreye, Emily Kame 32-33
Kusama, Yayoi 125

landscapes 20-33, 41, 46, 53, 64, 66, 69, 110, 120
leisure 104, 116, 117
Lichtenstein, Roy 59
lions 34-35, 40-41, 44
love 28, 49, 60, 64, 72, 82, 86, 109, 124

Malevich, Kazimir 123
Manet, Edouard 53, 121
Marc, Franz 46-47, 97
Matisse, Henri 58, 59
memoirs 80
men 66, 78, 82, 93, 98, 112, 121
Merian, Maria Sybilla 38-39
Metsys, Quentin 90-91
Mexico / Mexican 98
Michelangelo 122
Millais, John Everett 94-95
Millet, Jean-François 96
Miró, Joan 72, 73
Modigliani, Amedeo 124
Monet, Claude 26-27, 53, 114
money 90, 102-103, 117
Morisot, Berthe 124
mountains 20, 22, 24, 28, 30, 47, 68-69, 76
Mozambique 88
Munch, Edvard 122
murals 84, 98-99, 100
music 28, 29, 73, 122
myths 20, 62, 66, 68, 96

Naïve art 44, 45, 97
nature 20, 22, 31, 33, 36, 38, 39, 41, 42, 44, 46, 47, 64, 65, 80, 106
Neel, Alice 18-19, 109
Neoclassicism 76
Nigeria 60

Oldenburg, Claes 120
O'Keeffe, Georgia 30-31

Patinir, Joachim 20-21
Perry, Grayson 74-75
photographs 11, 25, 31, 60, 102
Picasso, Pablo 12, 56, 57, 84-85
plants 32, 38, 60, 80, 106
play 104-117
politics 8, 10, 11, 80, 97, 121
Pop Art 59, 120
portraits 6-19, 40, 54, 74, 125
Portugal 37, 88
power 10-11, 32, 34, 36, 40, 41, 42, 80, 88, 112
Pre-Raphaelites 83, 94-95
printing / prints 11, 25, 37, 38
public art 99, 100-101

Qichang, Dong 120
queens 10, 12, 14

religion 21, 44-45, 46, 60, 64-65, 82, 90, 94-95, 96, 97, 122
Rembrandt 14, 92-93
Renaissance 16, 65, 94
Ringgold, Faith 86-87
Rivera, Diego 98-99
rivers 20-21, 36, 66
Romans 8, 16, 20, 37, 76
Romanticism 22, 41
Russia / Russian 28, 97

saints 64-65, 74, 97
Sargent, John Singer 114-115
Savage, Augusta 16-17
science 34-35, 38, 39, 65, 79, 80, 116
scrolls 8, 68-69, 106
sculptures 16, 87, 88, 100-101, 104-105, 122, 124
sea 22, 26, 42, 50, 66, 82
self-portraits 14-15
Seurat, George 116, 117
sisters 18, 108-109, 114
sketches 34-35
soldiers 23, 76, 78-79, 85, 100, 123, 124
South America 6, 38
Spain / Spanish 10, 12, 72, 77, 84, 112
spiritual 28, 32-33, 36, 42, 46-47, 65, 69, 90-91, 122
sports 104, 107, 110
still lifes 42, 48-61, 75, 90, 120
stories / storytelling 16, 44, 62-75, 78, 79, 82, 86, 120
Stubbs, George 40-41, 44, 105
sun 23, 26, 28, 48, 62, 66, 114
Surrealism 73

tapestries 75, 78, 79, 112
tigers 42, 44, 69
trade 90, 100, 102-103
trees 21, 24, 28, 42, 69, 108, 110
Turner, J M W 22, 23

Uccello, Paulo 79, 95
United States / USA 11, 30, 86, 98, 101, 116
unknown artists 6, 8, 10, 36, 48, 62, 78, 104, 124

Velázquez, Diego 12-13
Vermeer, Johannes 123
Vigée Le Brun, Elizabeth 14-15
da Vinci, Leonardo 34-35, 38, 95

wars 23, 84-85, 88, 100
wealth 8, 10, 11, 46, 62, 64, 90-91, 109
weapons 80, 88
Wearing, Gillian 121
weather 20, 24, 26-27, 30, 96
Whistler, James Abbott McNeill 122
women 8, 12, 15, 32, 38, 39, 49, 62, 69, 78, 82, 84, 86, 90, 96-97, 98, 108-109, 112, 121, 124, 125
work 18, 39, 46, 66, 68, 82, 90-103, 116

Zhong, Zheng 43, 68-69

To my darling Andrew - I.S.
In memory of my grandmother Frances Cooke, who started me on my journey of taking great art apart - M.A.

First published in 2022 by Wayland

With thanks for the advice and support of Andrew Wilson, former Senior Curator at Tate Britain

Edited by Rachel Cooke and Paul Rockett
Design by Pony Ltd., London
Cover montage by Niall Sweeney
Picture research by Diana Morris

Printed in China

Wayland, an imprint of Hachette Children's Group
Part of Hodder and Stoughton
Carmelite House
50 Victoria Embankment
London EC4Y 0DZ

An Hachette UK Company
www.hachette.co.uk
www.hachettechildrens.co.uk

ISBN 978 1 5263 1494 9
ISBN 978 1 5263 1495 6

FSC
www.fsc.org
MIX
Paper from responsible sources
FSC® C104740

Picture credits

Front cover: tl. Wassily Kandinsky, *Composition IV*, 1911, detail. Oil on canvas, 159.5 × 250.5 cm. Kunstsammlungen Nordrhein-Westfalen, Düsseldorf, Germany. Luisa Ricciarini/Bridgeman Images.
tcl. Egyptian maker unknown, *Hippopotamus*, 1961-1878BCE, detail. Faience, 11.2 × 7.5 × 20 cm. Metropolitan Museum of Art, New York, USA, gift Edward S. Harkness.
tc. Elisabeth Louise Vigée Le Brun, *Self-Portrait in a Straw Hat*, 1782, detail. Oil on canvas, 97.8 × 27.7 cm. National Gallery, London, UK. AKG Images.
tcr. Augusta Christine (Fells) Savage, *Portrait Head of John Henry*, c.1940, detail. Patinated plaster, 16.8 × 8.9 × 12.1 cm. Museum of Fine Arts, Boston, USA. The John Axelrod Collection - Frank B. Bemis Fund, Charles H. Bayley Fund and The Heritage Fund for a Diverse Collection.
c. Anon, *Portrait of Terentius Neo and His Wife*, c.79CE, detail. Fresco from Pompeii, 65 × 58 cm. Naples Archaeological Museum, Naples, Italy. Dmitriy Moroz/iStock.
cb. Anon, *Armada Portrait of Elizabeth I*, c.1588, detail. Oil on oak panel, 110.5 × 125 cm. Royal Museums Greenwich, UK. Stefano Ravero/Queen's House Greenwich/Alamy.
cbr. Anon, Cueva de los Manos, Argentina c.8000BCE. Sprayed pigments, hand stencils on rock. Edouardo Rivero/Shutterstock.
bl. Jacques-Louis David, *Napoleon Crossing the Alps*, 1801, detail. Oil on canvas, 273 × 234 cm. Palace of Versailles, France. Google Cultural Institute/Wikimedia Commons/PD.
br. Albrecht Dürer, *Rhinoceros*, 1515, detail. Woodcut, 23.5 × 29.8 cm. This version National Gallery of Art, Washington DC, USA. NGA/Wikimedia Commons/PD.

4tl. Anon, *The Bayeux Tapestry*, around 1070s, detail, Wool thread on linen, 70 × 50 m. Bayeux Museum, Bayeux, France. Jorisvo/Shutterstock.
4c. Grayson Perry, *The Annunciation of the Virgin Deal*, 2012, detail. Tapestry, 200 × 400 cm. Arts Council Collection, London, UK. © The Artist, courtesy of Victoria Miro Gallery, London, UK.
4bl. Jean-François Millet, *The Gleaners*, 1857, detail. Oil on canvas, 84 × 112 cm. Musée d'Orsay, Paris, France. Google Art Project/Wikimedia Commons/PD.
5tl. John Singer Sargent, *Carnation, Lily, Lily, Rose*, 1885-86, detail. Oil on canvas, 174 × 153.7 cm. Tate Britain, London. Painting/Alamy.
5tr. Katsushika Hokusai, *Ejiri in Suruga Province*, 1830-32, detail. Woodblock print, 25.1 × 37.5 cm. Metropolitan Museum of Art, New York, USA. Henry L Phillips Collection/PD.
5c. Egyptian maker unknown, *Hippopotamus*, 1961-1878BCE, detail. Faience, 11.2 x.7.5 × 20 cm. Metropolitan Museum of Art New York, USA, gift Edward S. Harkness.
5b. Vincent van Gogh, *Sunflowers*, 1888, detail. Oil on canvas, 92.1 × 73 cm. National Gallery, London, UK. Jenya/Alamy.
6-7. Anon, Cueva de los Manos, Argentina, c.8000BCE. Sprayed pigments, hand stencils on rock. **6cl, 6b, 7b** Tony Kallman; **6cr** R. M. Nunes; **7t** Edouardo Rivero/Shutterstock.
8-9. Anon, *Portrait of Terentius Neo and His Wife*, c.79CE. Fresco from Pompeii, 65 × 58 cm. Naples Archaeological Museum, Naples, Italy. Dmitriy Moroz/iStock.
10. Anon, *Armada Portrait of Elizabeth I*, c.1588. Oil on oak panel, 110.5 × 125 cm. Royal Museums Greenwich, UK. Stefano Ravero/Queen's House, Greenwich/Alamy.
11. Shepard Fairey, *Barack Obama*, 2008. Hand-finished collage, stencil, and acrylic on heavy paper, 152.4 × 111.76 cm. National Portrait Gallery, Smithsonian Institution, gift of the Heather and Tony Podesta Collection in honor of Mary K. Podesta. © Shephard Fairey/ObeyGiant.com.
12-13. Diego Velázquez, *Las Meninas*, 1656. Oil on canvas, 318 × 276 cm. Museo del Prado, Madrid, Spain. Google Earth/Wikimedia Commons/PD.
14-15. Elisabeth Louise Vigée Le Brun, *Self Portrait in a Straw Hat*, 1782. Oil on canvas, 97.8 × 27.7 cm. National Gallery, London, UK. AKG Images.
16-17. Augusta Christine (Fells) Savage, *Portrait Head of John Henry*, c.1940. Patinated plaster, 16.8 × 8.9 × 12.1 cm. Museum of Fine Arts, Boston, USA. The John Axelrod Collection - Frank B. Bemis Fund, Charles H. Bayley Fund and The Heritage Fund for a Diverse Collection.
18-19. Alice Neel, *The De Vegh Twins*, 1975. Oil on canvas, 121.92 × 101.6 cm. David Zwirner © Alice Neel Estate.
20-21. Joachim Patinir, *Landscape with Charon Crossing the Styx*, 1520-1524. Oil on wood panel, 64 × 103 cm. Museo del Prado, Madrid, Spain. Wikimedia Commons/PD.
22. Caspar David Friedrich, *Wanderer Above the Sea of Fog*, c.1818. Oil on canvas, 94.8 × 74.8 cm. Kunsthalle Hamburg, Germany. cybershot8000i/Wikimedia Commons/PD.
23. J M W Turner, *Snow Storm: Hannibal and his Army Crossing the Alps*, 1812. Oil paint on canvas, 146 × 237.5 cm. Tate Britain, London, UK. ArtHeritage/Alamy.
24-25. Katsushika Hokusai, *Ejiri in Suruga Province*, 1830-32. Woodblock print, 25.1 × 37.5 cm. Metropolitan Museum of Art, New York, USA. Henry L. Phillips Collection/PD.
26-27. Claude Monet, *Impression, Sunrise*, 1872. Oil on canvas, 46 × 64 cm. Musée Marmottan, Paris, France. Wikimedia Commons/PD.
28-29. Wassily Kandinsky, *Composition IV*, 1911. Oil on canvas, 159.5 × 250.5 cm. Kunstsammlungen Nordrhein-Westfalen, Düsseldorf, Germany. Luisa Ricciarini/Bridgeman Images.
30-31. Georgia O'Keeffe, *Black Mesa Landscape, New Mexico*, 1930. Oil on canvas mounted on board, 62 × 90 cm. Georgia O'Keeffe Museum, Santa Fe, New Mexico, USA. © DACS 2022. Albert Knapp/Alamy.
32-33. Emily Kame Kngwarreye, *Ntange Dreaming*, 1989. Synthetic Polymer paint on canvas, 135 × 122 cm. National Gallery of Australia, Canberra/Bridgeman Images London. © The artist/DACS 2022.
34-35. Leonardo da Vinci, *Cats, Lions and a Dragon*, c.1517. Black chalk, pen and ink wash on paper, 27 × 21 cm. Royal Collection Trust, UK. Denis Halinan/Alamy.
36. Egyptian maker unknown, *Hippopotamus*, 1961-1878BCE. Faience, 11.2 x.7.5 × 20 cm. Metropolitan Museum of Art New York, USA, gift Edward S. Harkness.
37. Albrecht Dürer, *Rhinoceros*, 1515. Woodcut, 23.5 × 29.8 cm. This version National Gallery of Art, Washington DC, USA. NGA/Wikimedia Commons/PD.
38-39. Maria Sibylla Merian, *Spectacled Caiman with South American False Coral Snake*, c.1705. Copper engraving and watercolour from *Metamorphosis insectorum Surinamensium*. Sepia Times/UIG/Getty Images.
40-41. George Stubbs, *Lion Attacking a Horse*, c.1765. Oil on canvas, 69 × 100.1 cm. National Gallery of Victoria, Melbourne, Australia/Bridgeman Images.
42-43. Tani Bunchō, *Tiger Family and Magpies*, 1807. Ink and colour on silk handing scroll, 157.3 × 85.7 cm. Los Angeles County Museum of Art, USA, gift of Charlotte Wayne and Richard Wayne in memory of Lenore Wayne/PD.
44-45. Edward Hicks, *Noah's Ark*, 1846. Oil on canvas, 66.8 × 77.2 cm. Philadelphia Museum of Art, USA. Wikimedia Commons/Google Cultural Institute/PD.
46-47. Franz Marc, *The Yellow Cow*, 1911. Oil on canvas, 140.5 × 189.2 cm. Solomon R. Guggenheim Museum, New York, USA. Album/Alamy.
48-49. Michelangelo di Caravaggio, *Still Life with Flowers and Fruit*, 1601. Oil on canvas, 184 × 105 cm. Ministero per i beni e le attività culturali, Galleria Borghese, Rome, Italy.
50-51. Jean-Baptiste Chardin, *The Ray*, 1728. Oil on canvas, 114 × 146 cm. Louvre, Paris, France. agefotostock/Alamy.
52-53. Paul Cézanne, *The Black Marble Clock*, 1869. Oil on canvas, 55.2 × 74.3 cm. Private Collection. The Yorck Project/Wikimedia Commons/PD.
54-55. Vincent van Gogh, *Sunflowers*, 1888. Oil on canvas, 92.1 × 73 cm. National Gallery, London, UK. Jenya/Alamy.
56-57. Georges Braque, *Still Life: Le Jour*, 1929. Oil on canvas, 115 × 146.7 cm. National Gallery of Art, Washington DC, USA.
58. Henri Matisse, *Red Interior, Still Life on a Blue Table*, 1947. Oil on canvas, 116 × 89 cm. © 2021 Kunstsammlung Nordrhein-Westfalen, Düsseldorf, Germany. © Succession H. Matisse/DACS London 2022. Bridgeman Images.
59. Roy Lichtenstein, *Still Life with Crystal Bowl*, 1972. Oil and magna on canvas, 132.1 × 106.7 cm. Whitney Museum of American Art, New York, USA. © Estate of Roy Lichtenstein/DACS, London 2022. The Lichtenstein Foundation/Artimage.
60-61. Njideka Akunyili Crosby, *Grandmother's Parlour*, 2016. Acrylic, transfers and coloured pencil on paper, 155.45 × 131.98 cm. Courtesy of the artist, Victoria Miro and David Zwirner © Njideka Akunyili Crosby. Photo credit Brian Forrest.
62-63. Anon, *Painted panel of Tatiaset*, c.825-71BCE. Gesso, paint on wood, h 23.4 cm. Metropolitan Museum of Art, New York, USA/PD.
64-65. Giovanni Bellini, *St Francis in Ecstasy*, 1476-78. Oil and tempera on wooden panel, 124.6 × 142 cm. Frick Collection, New York, USA. Google Cultural Institute/Wikimedia commons/PD.
66-67. Pieter Bruegel the Elder, *Landscape with the Fall of Icarus*, c.1560. Oil on canvas, 73.5 × 112cm. Musées Royaux des Beaux-Arts de Belgique, Brussels, Belgium. Bridgeman Images.
68-69. Zheng Zhong, *Searching the Mountains for Demons*, c.1618-48. Ink and colour on paper scroll, 27 × 847.1 cm. Metropolitan Museum of Art, New York, USA/Bequest of Dorothy Graham Bennett, 1991/PD.
70-71. Sahib Din, 'Indrajit meets with Ravana', from *The Mewar Ramayana*, Add.15297(1), f.34 rc. 1650-52. Watercolour on paper, 22.86 × 39 cm. © British Library Board/Bridgeman Images.
72. Joan Miró, *Carnival of Harlequin*, 1924-25. Oil on canvas, 66.04 × 93 cm. Albright-Knox Art Gallery, Buffalo, New York, USA. © Successió Miró S.L/DACS, London 2022.
73. Dorothea Tanning, *Eine Kleine Nachtmusik*, 1943. Oil on canvas, 40.7 × 61 cm. Tate Modern, London, UK. © DACS, London 2022.
74-75. Grayson Perry, *The Annunciation of the Virgin Deal*, 2012. Tapestry, 200 × 400 cm. Arts Council Collection, London, UK. © The Artist, courtesy of Victoria Miro Gallery, London, UK.
76-77. Jacques-Louis David, *Napoleon Crossing the Alps*, 1801. Oil on canvas, 273 × 234 cm. Palace of Versailles, France. Google Cultural Institute/Wikimedia Commons/PD.
78. Anon, *The Bayeux Tapestry*, around 1070s, detail. Wool thread on linen, 70 × 50 m. Bayeux Museum, Bayeux, France. Jorisvo/Shutterstock
79. Paulo Uccello, *The Battle of San Romano* c.1438-40. Tempera on wood, 182 × 320 cm. National Gallery, London, UK. Bridgeman Images.
80-81. Farrukh Beg, *Babur Receives a Courtier*, 1589. Opaque watercolor and gold on paper, 41.4. × 27 cm. Sackler Gallery, Freer Gallery of Art, Washington DC, USA.
82-83. Ford Madox Brown, *The Last of England*, 1855. Oil on panel, 82.5 × 75 cm. Birmingham Museums and Art Gallery, Birmingham, UK. Wikipedia commons/PD.
84-85. Pablo Picasso, *Guernica*, 1937. Oil on canvas, 349.3 × 776 cm. Museo Nacional Centro de Arte Reina Sofia, Madrid, Spain. © Succession Picasso/DACS, London 2022/Bridgeman Images.
86-87. Faith Ringgold, *The Sunflower Quilting Bee at Arles*, 1991. Colour litho, 71.1 × 76.2 cm. Private Collection. Courtesy of the artist's studio. © DACS, London 2022.
88-89. Cristóvão Canhavato (Kester), *Throne of Weapons*, 2001. Decommissioned weapons from Mozambique, 101 × 66 × 80 cm. © Cristóvão Canhavato. Photo © Trustees of The British Museum, London.
90-91. Quentin Metsys, *The Moneylender and His Wife*, 1514. Oil on panel, 70 × 67 cm. Musée du Louvre, Paris, France. The Yorck Project/Wikimedia Commons/PD.
92-93. Rembrandt, *The Anatomy Lesson of Dr Nicolaes Tulp*, 1632. Oil on canvas, 216.5 × 169.5 cm. Museum Mauritshuis, The Hague, Netherlands. Wikimedia Commons/PD.
94-95. John Everett Millais, *Christ in the House of His Parents*, 1849-50. Oil on canvas, 86.4 × 139.7 cm. Tate Britain, London, UK. Artepics/Superstock.
96. Jean-François Millet, *The Gleaners*, 1857. Oil on canvas, 84 × 112 cm. Musée d'Orsay, Paris, France. Google Art Project/Wikimedia Commons/PD
97. Natalia Goncharova, *Gardening*, 1908. Oil on canvas, 102.9 × 123.2 cm. Tate Britain, London, UK/© DACS, London 2022.
98-99. Diego Rivera, *The Making of a Fresco Showing the Building of a City*, 1931. Tempera onto lime plaster. San Francisco Art Institute, USA. Photo credit © Jay Galvin. © Estate of Diego Rivera, Banco do Mexico and Instituto Naçional de Bellas Artes y Literatura, Mexico.
100-101. Jonathan Borofsky, *Hammering Man*, 1990. Monumental kinetic sculpture, painted steel in Frankfurt, Germany. Uwe Aranas/Alamy.
102-103. Andreas Gursky, *Chicago, Board of Trade II*, 1999. Photograph, colour, chromogenic print on paper, 157.4 × 284 cm. Tate Modern, London, UK. © Courtesy Monika Sprüth Galerie, Köln/VG Bild-Kunst, Bonn and DACS, London 2022.
104-105. Anon, *The Jockey of Artemision*, c.150-140BCE. Bronze, ciré perdue method, 210 × 290 cm. Hercules Milas/Alamy.
106-107. Su Hanchen, *One Hundred Children in the Long Spring*, c.1150. Song Dynasty. Scroll, ink and colours on silk. Wikimedia Commons/Tonloe5533/CC BY SA 4.0. and The Picture Art Collection/Alamy.
108-109. Sofonisba Anguissola, *The Chess Game*, 1555. Oil on canvas, 72 × 97 cm. Museum Narodowe, Poznan, Poland/Bridgeman Images.
110-111. Hendrick Avercamp, *Winter Landscape with Ice Skaters*, 1608. Oil on oak, 77.3 × 131.9 cm. Rijksmuseum, Amsterdam, Netherlands. Wikimedia Commons CC0 1.0/PD.
112-113. Francisco de Goya, *The Straw Manikin*, 1791-92. Oil on canvas, 267 × 160 cm. Museo del Prado, Madrid, Spain. A. Burkatovski/Superstock.
114-115. John Singer Sargent, *Carnation, Lily, Lily, Rose*, 1885-86, detail. Oil on canvas, 174 × 153.7 cm. Tate Britain, London. Painting/Alamy.
116. George Seurat, *A Sunday Afternoon on the Island of La Grande Jatte*, 1884-86. Oil on canvas, 207.6 × 308 cm. Art Institute of Chicago, USA. Google Art Institute/Wikimedia Commons/PD.
117. Kerry James Marshall, *Past Times*, 1997. Acrylic and collage on canvas, 289.6 × 396.2 cm. David Zwirner/Private Collection. © The artist.
120t. Claes Oldenburg and Coosje van Bruggen, *Spoonbridge and Cherry*, 1988. Stainless steel and aluminium, 900 × 400.1 cm. Minneapolis Sculpture Garden, Minneapolis, USA. Shutterstock.
120bl. Giovanna Garzoni, *Still Life with Bowl of Citrons*, late 1640s. Tempera on vellum, 27.6 × 35.6 cm. J. Paul Getty Museum, Los Angeles, California, USA. CCA 4.0 International Licence.
120br. Dong Qichong, *Landscape with Calligraphy*, c.1555-1636. Ink and pigments on paper. Tokyo National Museum, Japan. Wikimedia Commons/PD.
121tl. El Greco (Doménikos Theotókopoulos), *View of Toledo*, c.1599-1600. Oil on canvas, 121.3 × 108.6 cm. Metropolitan Museum of Art, New York, USA/PD.
121tr. Edouard Manet, *A Bar at the Folies-Bergère*, 1882. Oil on canvas, 96 × 103 cm. Courtauld Gallery, London, UK. Fondation Vuitton, Paris/Wikimedia Commons CCA 2.0.
121bl. Hans Holbein the Younger, *The Ambassadors*, 1533. Oil on oak panel, 207 × 209.5 cm. National Gallery, London, UK. Ian Dagnall/Alamy.
121br. Gillian Wearing, *Millicent Garrett Fawcett*, 2018. Bronze. Cabral Correia/Shutterstock.
122tl. Gechū, active 18th century, *Baku: Monster that Eats Nightmares*. Netsuke, Ivory and pigment, 9.5 × 4.1 × 3 cm. Los Angeles County Museum, Los Angeles, California, USA/PD.
122tc. Edvard Munch, *The Scream*, 1893. Oil, pastel and tempera on cardboard, 91 × 73.4 cm. Nasjonalgaleriet, Oslo, Norway/Denis Hallinan/Alamy.
122tr. James McNeill Whistler, *Nocturne in Blue and Gold, Old Battersea Bridge*, 1872-75. Oil on canvas, 68 × 51 cm. Tate Britain, London, UK. The Yorck Project/Wikimedia Commons/PD.
122bl. John Constable, *The Hay Wain*, 1821. Oil on canvas. 130 × 185 cm. National Gallery, London, UK. Ivy Close Images/Alamy.
122br. Michelangelo, *Pieta*, 1498-99. Marble, 174 × 195 cm. St Peter's Basilica, Vatican City. Fotofires/Shutterstock.
123tl. Gustav Klimt, *The Kiss*, 1907-08. Oil on canvas, added gold leaf, silver and platinum. 180 × 180 cm. Galerie Belvedere, Vienna, Austria. Google Cultural Institute/Wikimedia commons/PD.
123tr. Johannes Vermeer, *The Milkmaid*, c.1660. Oil on canvas, 45.5 × 41 cm. Rijksmuseum, Amsterdam, Netherlands. Google Art Project/Wikimedia commons/PD.
123bl. Kazimir Malevich, *Red Cavalry Riding*, 1928-32. Oil on canvas, 91 × 140 cm. Russian Museum, St Petersburg, Russia. Wikimedia commons/PD.
123br. Angelica Kauffman, *The Sorrow of Telemachus*, 1783. Oil on canvas, 83.2cm × 114.3 cm. Metropolitan Museum of Art, New York, USA/PD.
124tl. Paul Gauguin, *Arearea*, 1892. Oil on canvas, 75 × 93 cm. Musée d'Orsay, Paris, France. Masterpics/Alamy.
124tr. Anon, Terracotta Army of Qin Shin Huang, Xian, China, c.210BCE. Ben Jeayes/Shutterstock.
124bl. Berthe Morisot, *The Cradle*, 1872. Oil on canvas, 56 × 46 cm. Musée d'Orsay, Paris, France. Google Cultural Project/Wikimedia Commons/PD.
124bc. Anon, Benin bronze head of an Oba, 18th century, Courtesy of the University of Aberdeen, Scotland.
124br. Amedeo Modigliani, *Portrait of the Artist's Wife*, 1918. Oil on canvas, 100.3 × 64.5 cm. Norton Simon Museum, Pasadena, California, USA. Wikimedia Commons/PD.
125tl. Yayoi Kusama, Yellow Pumpkin, Naoshima, Japan, 1994. Cast steel. Carlos Huang/Shutterstock.
125tr. Artemisia Gentileschi, *Judith and Her Maidservant with the Head of Holofernes*, c.1623-25. Oil on canvas, 72.44 × 55.75 cm. Detroit Institute of Arts, Detroit, USA. Wikimedia Commons/PD.
125bl. Jan van Eyck, *The Arnolfini Portrait*, 1434. Oil on oak panel, 82 × 60 cm. National Gallery, London, UK. Giorgio Morara/Alamy.
125br. Louise Bourgeois, *Mamam*, 1999. Stainless steel, bronze, marble. 927 × 891 × 1,024 cm. Guggenheim Bilbao, Spain. Shell300/Shutterstock.

Every attempt has been made to clear copyright. Should there be any inadvertent omission please apply to the publisher for rectification.